Carolyn's Paper-Pieced

Garden

Beloved historic patterns for miniature and full-sized quilts.

On the cover and above: Carolyn's Paper-Pieced Garden designed and made
by Carolyn Cullinan McCormick and quilted by Tracy Peterson Yadon,
Lady Quilter, of Manhattan, Montana.

by Carolyn Cullinan McCormick

Carolyn's Paper-Pieced Garden

Beloved historic patterns for miniature and full-size quilts.

By **Carolyn Cullinan McCormick**
Edited by **Edie McGinnis**, KC Star
Photography by Bill Krzyzanowski
Book Design by Cheryl Davis, *c davis creative*

Published by KANSAS CITY STAR BOOKS
1729 Grand Boulevard
Kansas City, Missouri 64108

First Edition

Library of Congress Card Number: 2003104034
ISBN 0-9740009-0-6

Printed in the United States of America
by Walsworth Publishing Co.

To order copies, call StarInfo 816.234.4636

www.TheKansasCityStore.com

www.PickleDish.com

The quilt above is Carolyn's Paper-Pieced Garden set together using the 4" blocks as cornerstones in the sashing. The quilt blocks were made by some of the ladies from the Quilters' Guild of Greater Kansas City. (Please see the acknowledgments for a complete list of names.) It was sewn together by Corky and Peggy Hutinett of Raytown, Missouri.

Carolyn's Paper-Pieced

Garden

Acknowledgments

I have so many people to thank for this book. Without their help and expertise I would never have been able to put this all together.

I appreciate the opportunity that was given to me by Doug Weaver from *The Kansas City Star* to transform the wonderful patterns from the past into the technique of the future.

I especially want to thank my editor, Edie McGinnis, also of *The Kansas City Star*, for her advice and help.

I owe my friend Diane Donnelly of Bozeman, Montana, a very big thank you for answering questions and for starting me on the road to quilting. A special thank you to Tracy Peterson Yadon, Lady Quilter, of Manhattan, Montana. You really came through for me in a pinch. Thanks also to my wonderful family and friends who took time to make quilts or test blocks for this book: Marie Huber, Glendive, Montana; Megan Netwal, Parker, Colorado; Patty Struck, Billings, Montana; Judy Schwender, Lincoln, Nebraska; Debbie Dent, Bozeman, Montana; Patrice Heath, Parker, Colorado; and Sandy Taylor, Bozeman, Montana.

Thanks to the wonderful ladies of the Quilters' Guild of Greater Kansas City who helped test blocks; Marion Murphy, Judy Lovell, Ann Bingham, Carol Kuse, Bami Drinkwater, Jan Keeler, Norma Niedner, Mary Ellen Bloomquist, Gloria Caruthers, Barbara Miller, Brenda Butcher, Dee Clevenger, Alta Short, Netta Ranney and Jan Jarchow. Thanks also go to the ladies from Quilter's Station of Lee's Summit, Missouri: Rita Briner, Jane Miller and Mary Andrews. Thank you Corky and Peggy Hutinett for sewing the blocks together and plucking off paper so the quilt from Kansas City could be photographed in time for this book.

Thanks to Cheryl Davis, of *c davis creative*, for her lovely design work on this book and to Bill Krzyzanowski, our photographer, for the great photos.

Table of Contents

Carolyn's Paper-Pieced Garden

Carolyn Cullinan McCormick

I was born and raised on a ranch near Glendive, Montana, and currently live in Franktown, Colorado. I have been married to my wonderful husband Larry for 27 years. We have two fabulous children, even though you can't call them children anymore, Ryan, 24, and Jennifer, 20. Ryan works as a junior analyst for a financial company in Denver and Jennifer is on a soccer scholarship at Hastings College in Nebraska. The baby of the family is our dog Jake, a 2 1/2 year old English Pointer.

Quilting has been a part of my life for 18 years. I worked and taught a variety of quilting and craft classes at the Patchworks in Bozeman, Montana, from 1987 to 1995. In 1995, out of frustration, I invented the Add-A-Quarter™ ruler.

The original idea for the Add-A-Quarter™ was to enable a person to automatically add a quarter inch to pieces cut with templates. This would allow one to use a rotary cutter to cut multiple pieces. Since the inception of paper-piecing, the ruler has taken on a whole new role in the quilting world and is a standard tool for making paper-pieced items. I have been distributing the Add-A-Quarter™ under my business name of CM Designs since 1996.

Quilting has taken me down many roads and given me the opportunity to meet many wonderful people!

I would like to dedicate this book to my family and thank them for their love and support.

Making a quilt is like working in your garden.

*C*hoosing your design or pattern is like the layout of your flower garden. Your fabric selection relates to the flower seeds you want to plant and the colors you like. Piecing your quilt is like planting your garden. It starts to take shape with each piece you add or each seed you plant.

There is a great sense of satisfaction when the garden seeds we have planted spring into new life. The flowers appear and we see and enjoy the fruits of our labor. As we add each piece of fabric to our quilt, it begins to grow just like our garden. The quilt blooms with color and spices up the home.

Both gardening and quilting can be hard work, but the pleasure we derive from the process far outweighs the time and labor involved.

I hope this book will help your ideas blossom and grow into a beautiful garden of quilts!

— *Carolyn Cullinan McCormick*

We invited our author, Carolyn Cullinan McCormick, to dig into the archives of *The Kansas City Star's* quilt patterns. While raking through the pages, she found a flowerpot, a cluster of lilies, a Missouri Daisy and many other patterns ready to spring into a fresh garden quilt.

You can make these blocks bloom as four-inch miniatures for a wall hanging or as a full-blown quilt using the ten-inch patterns. Whatever size you choose to make, Carolyn has made it easy for you by redrafting the patterns into today's method of foundation paper piecing. Amble through Carolyn's Paper-Pieced Garden and enjoy the sweet success of paper piecing these Kansas City Stars.

Why paper piece?

Paper piecing is great for beginners as well as experienced quilters. One can make a wonderful quilt on their very first try since complicated patterns are broken down into easily managed steps. Sewing the fabric to paper makes matching points relatively easy and the paper stabilizes the fabric, enabling one to use even the smallest of scraps.

How to paper piece:

Get ready...

1. Use a copy machine to copy your pattern. Make all of your copies from the same original and use the same copy machine. All copy machines distort to some extent so check your pattern by holding the original and the copy together with a light source behind the two sheets of paper. Make as many copies as necessary. It's nice to have a few extras in case you make an error. Use the lightest weight paper you can find. The heavier the paper, the more difficult it is to remove.

2. Set up your sewing machine. Use a 90/14 size needle and set the stitch length to 18-20 stitches per inch. The larger needle perforates the paper making it easier to tear off. The smaller stitches keep the seams from ripping out when you remove the paper.

3. Place a piece of muslin or scrap fabric on your ironing board. When you press the pieces, the ink from the copies can transfer onto your ironing board cover.

4. Make sure you have a light source nearby. The light on your sewing machine is usually adequate.

Get Set...

1. Here is a familiar pattern... see *Fig. A*, next page. Instead of templates with seam allowances as many of us are used to seeing, we have lines and numbers. The lines indicate where to sew and the numbers indicate the sequence in which to sew. The only seam allowances that are shown are the ones that go around either a block or a unit.

Paper-piecing how to's are continued on the next page

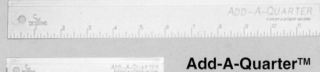

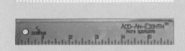

Add-A-Quarter™ and Add-An-Eighth™ Rulers

Paper-Piecing Supplies:

■ Add-A-Quarter™ Ruler – 10" Blocks

■ Add-An-Eighth™ Ruler – 4" Blocks

■ Rotary Cutter and Mat

■ Rulers for Rotary Cutting

■ Sewing Machine

■ 90/14 Sewing Machine Needles

■ Thread

■ Iron and Ironing Board

■ Straight Pins (Regular, Silk and/or Flower Head)

■ Double-Sided tape (Optional)

■ Index Card or a Piece of Template Plastic Measuring 3" x 10"

■ Tweezers (For removing small pieces of paper)

■ Paper for Foundation Piecing (This should be relatively thin)

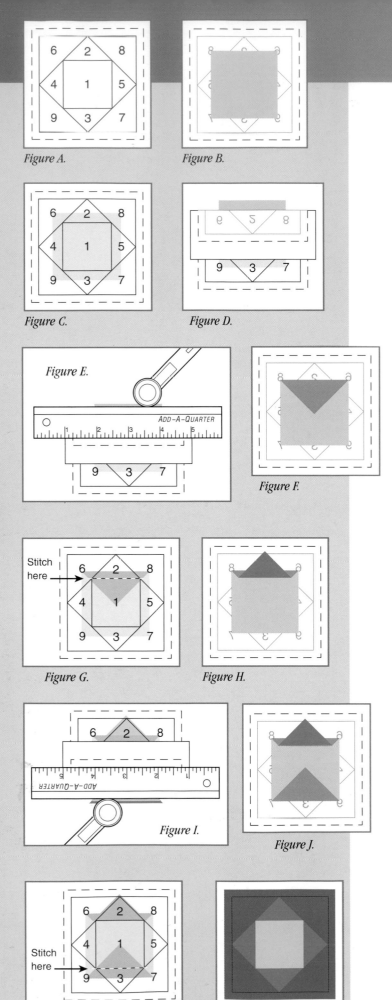

Figure A.

Figure B.

Figure C.

Figure D.

Figure E.

Figure F.

Figure G.

Figure H.

Figure I.

Figure J.

Figure K.

Figure L.

2. The front of the pattern is where the lines and numbers are printed. This is the side you will sew on.

3. The back of the pattern is the side that is blank. This is where your fabric will be placed.

4. Cut your fabric pieces by following the cutting chart for each block. Always make sure the piece of fabric is at least one-quarter of an inch larger all the way around than shown on the foundation pattern.

Sew!

1. Put fabric number 1 RIGHT SIDE UP on the blank side of the pattern. You may either pin the piece in place or use double-sided sticky tape to hold the fabric in place. The tape makes the fabric lie flat on the paper. The pin can make a small rise in the paper. See **Fig. B**, in the pictures at the left.

2. Turn the foundation pattern over, look through the paper toward your light source and make sure the fabric extends over the lines on each side by at least one-quarter of an inch. See **Fig. C**.

3. Place an index card or the template plastic on the sewing line between piece number 1 and piece number 2. Fold back the foundation pattern over the edge of the card. You can now see the excess fabric from piece number 1. See **Fig. D**.

4. Place the Add-A-Quarter ruler up against the fold of the foundation paper with the lip side down. Use a rotary cutter to trim the extra fabric from piece number 1. You will now have a straight line to help you place fabric piece number 2. See **Fig. E**.

5. Now place the fabric that goes in position number 2 of the pattern on the trimmed edge of piece number 1 with the right sides facing each other. See **Fig. F**.

6. Turn the foundation paper over and stitch on the line between piece number 1 and piece number 2. Sew a few stitches before the line begins and a few stitches after the line ends. Make sure piece number 2 does not slip. See **Fig. G**.

7. Flip the paper back over and open piece number 2. Press the piece open using a dry iron. See **Fig. H**.

8. Fold the foundation paper back along the line between piece number 1 and piece number 3 using the index card or the template plastic. Butt the Add-A-Quarter up against the paper and trim the excess fabric. See **Fig. I**.

9. Turn the foundation back over and position fabric piece number 3, being careful not to displace your fabric. Sew on the line between number 1 and number 3. See **Fig. J & K**.

10. Continue sewing each piece in place in the numeric order

given until all the pieces are sewn in place and each unit is complete. See **Fig. L**.

After all the pieces are sewn onto the foundation, you will be ready to trim the edges. You will need a 1/4" seam allowance around the entire block, no matter the size of the block, when you sew your blocks together. NEVER TRIM ON THE SOLID LINE! Line up the ruler with the solid line on the foundation. Trim off the excess fabric using your rotary cutter.

If you are paper piecing a block that is made up of multiple units, the time has come to sew them together. Either pin or baste the units together. Make sure the lines you are sewing match on the top and the bottom of the units. This can be accomplished by putting a pin straight through both lines at each intersection. Always check to make sure the seam is directly on the top line and the underneath line as well, otherwise your block will be off.

When the block is finished, DO NOT REMOVE THE PAPER! It is best to join the blocks before you remove the paper. This gives you a line to follow when you sew the blocks together. Remove the paper after all the blocks are sewn together. You might want to remove the really small pieces with a pair of tweezers.

A few variations...

Since these patterns from *The Kansas City Star* have been adapted to a paper pieced pattern from traditional blocks, you will have a few things crop up that you might not run into with blocks that were originally designed with paper piecing in mind.

1. You may have triangles that are either sewn to inside or outside corners of the block. These are shown as separated pieces. Machine-baste or pin your fabric to the triangles and sew them in the order indicated on the pattern leaving the paper in place.

2. Some portions are strip-pieced, then cut to fit the paper-pieced pattern. (See the Garden Walk block for an example.) You will find the pattern marked with double-pointed arrows.

3. Use half-square triangles where you see this symbol: ◣

Just a few suggestions...

If you have to unsew and the paper foundation separates on the sewing line, use a piece of clear tape to repair the pattern.

Sometimes you will notice the stitches from the previously sewn fabric when you fold back the foundation. If this happens, just pull the foundation away from the fabric and trim using the ruler.

The May Basket in Floral Tones wall hanging was made by Carolyn Cullinan McCormick.

Cluster of Lilies
December 1934
The Kansas City Star

From the floral fabric, cut:

■ One 1 3/4" x 14" strip. Subcut the strip into eight 1 3/4" squares. Cut the squares into half-square triangles.

■ One 1 1/2" x 6" strip. Subcut the strip into four 1 1/2" squares.

■ One 2 3/4" x 5 1/2" strip.

Subcut the strip into two 2 3/4" squares. Cut the squares into half-square triangles.

From the dark fabric, cut:

■ One 1 1/2" x 17" strip. Subcut the strip into eight 1 1/2" squares, one 1 1/2" x 3" rectangle and two 1" x 1 1/2" rectangles.

■ One 2" x 8" strip. Subcut the strip into four 2" squares. Cut the squares into half-square triangles.

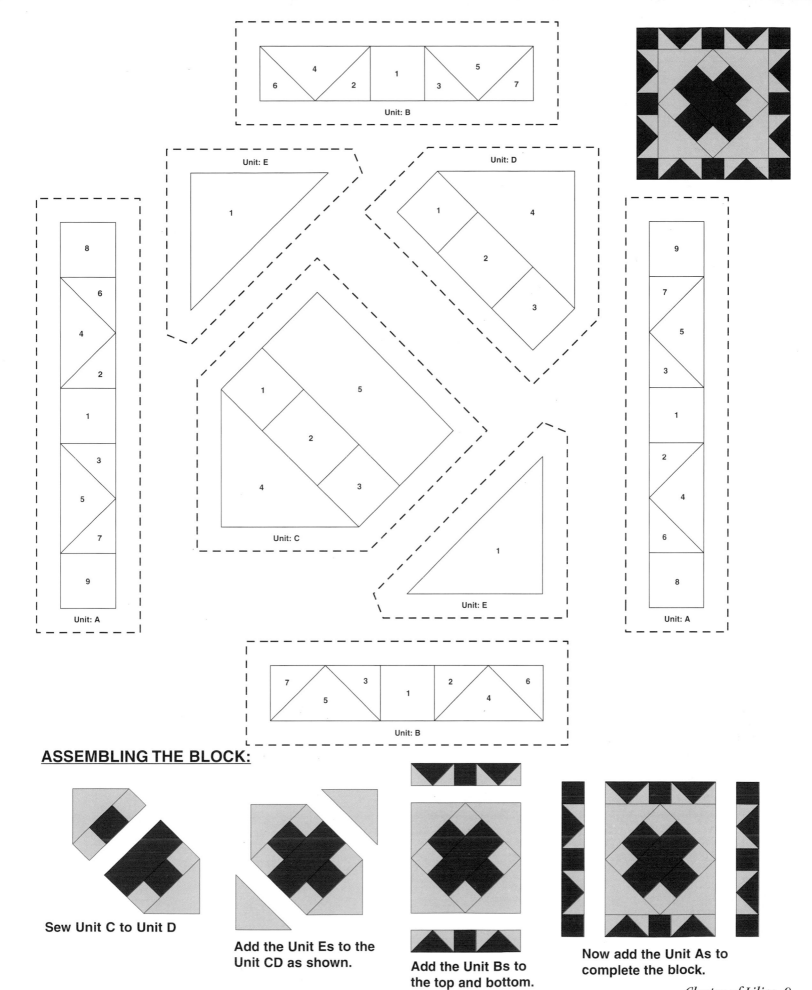

Unit: B

Unit: E

Unit: D

Unit: A

Unit: C

Unit: E

Unit: A

Unit: B

ASSEMBLING THE BLOCK:

Sew Unit C to Unit D

Add the Unit Es to the Unit CD as shown.

Add the Unit Bs to the top and bottom.

Now add the Unit As to complete the block.

Cluster of Lilies 9.

Cluster of Lilies
December 1934
The Kansas City Star

Position Chart — 4" Block

Fabric	Position #	Size	
Unit A – Make 2			
Dark	1,8,9	1 1/2" x 1 1/2"	
Floral	2,3,6,7	1 3/4" x 1 3/4"	◣
Dark	4,5	2" x 2"	◣
Unit B – Make 2			
Dark	1	1 1/2" x 1 1/2"	
Floral	2,3,6,7	1 3/4" x 1 3/4"	◣
Dark	4,5	2" x 2"	◣
Unit C – Make 1			
Floral	1,3	1 1/2" x 1 1/2"	
Dark	2	1" x 1 1/2"	
Floral	4	2 3/4" x 2 3/4"	◣
Dark	5	1 1/2" x 3"	
Unit D – Make 1			
Floral	1,3	1 1/2" x 1 1/2"	
Dark	2	1" x 1 1/2"	
Floral	4	2 3/4" x 2 3/4"	◣
Unit E – Make 2			
Floral	1	2 3/4" x 2 3/4"	◣

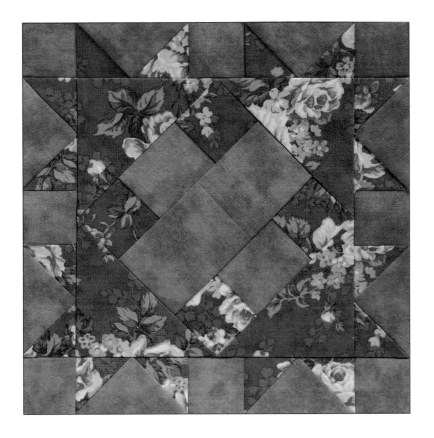

Cutting Directions – Cluster of Lilies 10" block

From the floral fabric, cut:

■ One 2 3/4" x 22" strip. Subcut the strip into eight 2 3/4" squares. Cut the squares into half-square triangles.

■ One 2 1/4" x 9" strip. Subcut the strip into four 2 1/4" squares.

■ One 5 1/4" x 10 1/2" strip. Subcut the strip into two 5 1/4" squares. Cut the squares into half-square triangles.

From the green fabric, cut:

■ One 2 1/4" x 18" strip. Subcut the strip into eight 2 1/4" squares.

■ One 3 1/2" x 14" strip. Subcut the strip into four 3 1/2" squares. Cut the squares into half-square triangles.

■ One 2 1/4" x 5 1/2" strip. Subcut the strip into two 2 1/4" x 2 3/4" rectangles.

■ One 2 3/4" x 6" strip.

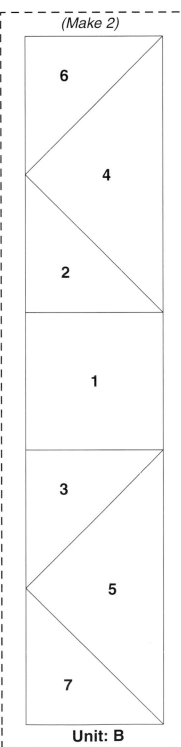

(Make 2)

Unit: B

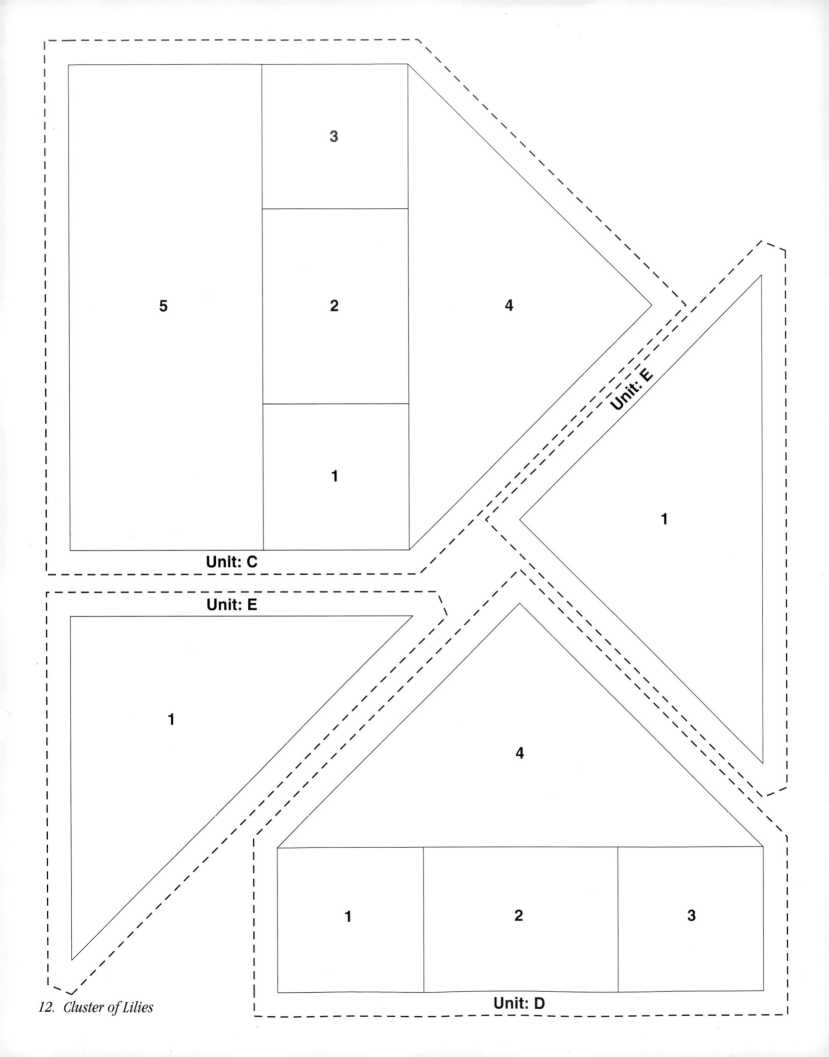

3

2

5

1

Unit: C

4

Unit: E

1

Unit: E

1

4

1

2

3

12. Cluster of Lilies

Unit: D

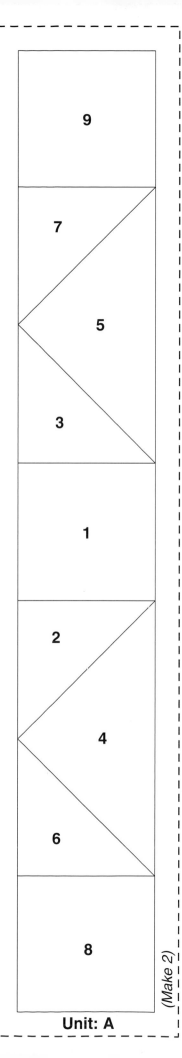

Unit: A

(Make 2)

Position Chart		10" Block
Fabric	**Position #**	**Size**
Unit A – Make 2		
Green Solid	1,8,9	2 1/4" x 2 1/4"
Floral	2,3,6,7	2 3/4" x 2 3/4"
Green Solid	4,5	3 1/2" x 3 1/2"
Unit B – Make 2		
Green Solid	1	2 1/4" x 2 1/4"
Floral	2,3,6,7	2 3/4" x 2 3/4"
Green Solid	4,5	3 1/2" x 3 1/2"
Unit C – Make 1		
Floral	1,3	2 1/4" x 2 1/4"
Green Solid	2	2 1/4" x 2 3/4"
Floral	4	5 1/4" x 5 1/4"
Green Solid	5	2 3/4" x 6"
Unit D – Make 1		
Floral	1,3	2 1/4" x 2 1/4"
Green Solid	2	2 1/4" x 2 3/4"
Floral	4	5 1/4" x 5 1/4"
Unit E – Make 2		
Floral	1	5 1/4" x 5 1/4"

When you are ready to sew the units together, refer to the instructions for the 4" block.

Leaves and Flowers
August 1935
The Kansas City Star

Cutting Directions — Leaves and Flowers 4" Block

From the floral fabric, cut:

■ One 2" x 6" strip. Subcut the strip into three 2" squares. Cut two of the squares into half-square triangles.

From the medium fabric, cut:

■ One strip 2" x 12." Subcut the strip into six 2" squares. Cut the squares into half-square triangles.

From the dark green fabric, cut:

■ One strip 1 3/4" x 7."

Subcut this strip into four 1 3/4" squares. Cut the squares into half-square triangles.

■ One 2 1/4" x 9" strip. Subcut the strip into four 2 1/4" squares.

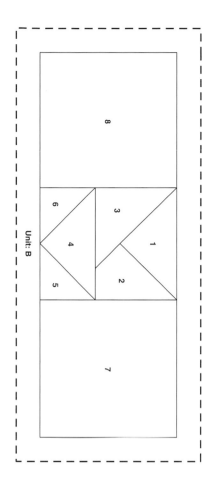

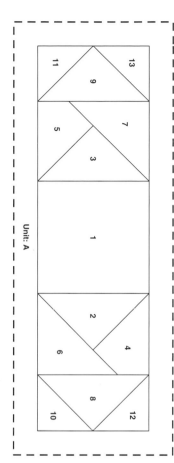

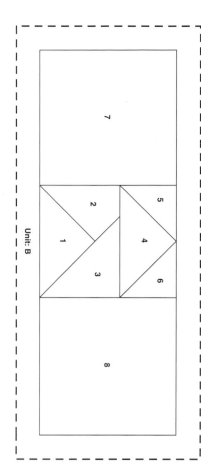

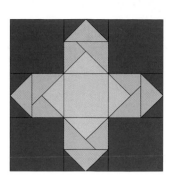

ASSEMBLING THE BLOCK:

Sew the Unit Bs to the top and bottom of the Unit A as shown to complete the block.

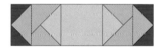

Position Chart	4" Block		
Fabric	**Position #**	**Size**	
Unit A – Make 1			
Floral	1	2" x 2"	
Floral	2,3	2" x 2"	◥
Medium	4,5,6,7,8,9	2" x 2"	◥
Dark Green	10,11,12,13	1 3/4" x 1 3/4"	◥
Unit B – Make 2			
Floral	1	2" x 2"	◥
Medium	2,3,4	2" x 2"	◥
Dark Green	5,6	1 3/4" x 1 3/4"	◥
Dark Green	7,8	2 1/4" x 2 1/4"	

Leaves and Flowers 15.

Leaves and Flowers
August 1935
The Kansas City Star

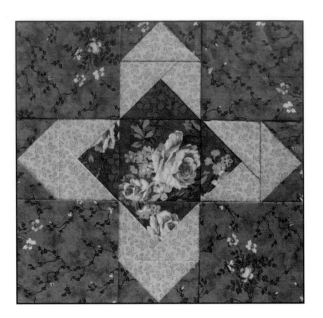

Cutting Directions — Leaves and Flowers 10" Block:

From the floral fabric, cut:

■ One 3 3/4" square.

■ One 3 1/2" x 7" strip. Subcut the 3 1/2" x 7" strip into two 3 1/2" squares. Cut the squares into half-square triangles.

From the yellow fabric, cut:

■ One 3 1/2" x 21" strip. Subcut the strip into six 3 1/2" squares. Cut the squares into half-square triangles.

From the green fabric, cut:

■ One 3" x 12" strip. Subcut the strip into four 3" squares. Cut the squares into half-square triangles.

■ One 4 1/2" x 18" strip. Subcut the strip into 4 1/2" squares.

When you are ready to sew the units together, refer to the instructions for the 4" block.

Fabric	Position #	Size	
Unit A – Make 1			
Floral	1	3 3/4" x 3 3/4"	
Floral	2,3	3 1/2" x 3 1/2"	◣
Yellow Leaves	4,5,6,7,8,9	3 1/2" x 3 1/2"	◣
Green Vine	10,11,12,13	3" x 3"	◣
Unit B – Make 2			
Floral	1	3 1/2" x 3 1/2"	◣
Yellow Leaves	2,3,4	3 1/2" x 3 1/2"	◣
Green Vine	5,6	3" x 3"	◣
Green Vine	7,8	4 1/2" x 4 1/2"	

Position Chart — 10" Block

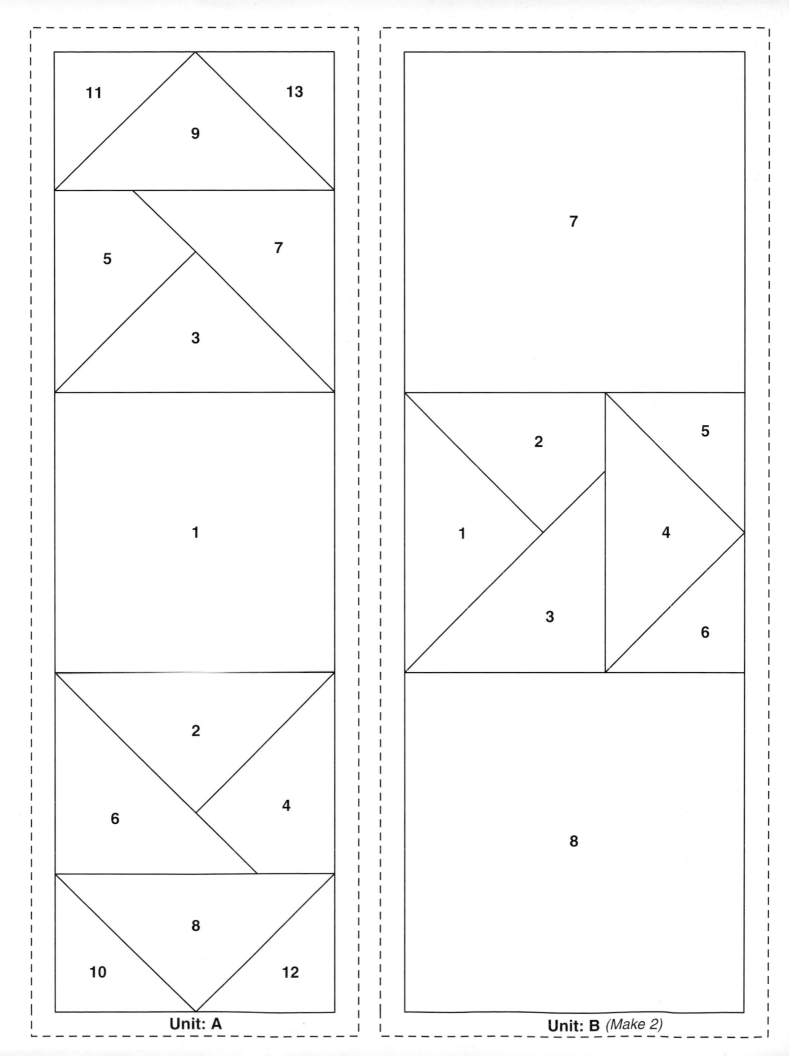

Unit: A

Unit: B *(Make 2)*

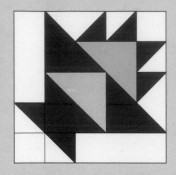

Flower Pot
January 1937
The Kansas City Star

From the light fabric, cut:

■ One 1 3/4" x 13" strip. Subcut the strip into four 1 3/4" squares and two 1 3/4" x 3" rectangles. Cut two of the 1 3/4" squares into half-square triangles.

■ One 2 1/2" square. Cut the square into half-square triangles.

From the dark green fabric, cut:

■ One 1 3/4" x 3 1/2" strip.

Subcut the strip into 1 3/4" squares. Cut the squares into half-square triangles.

From the medium fabric, cut:

■ One 3" square. Cut the square into half-square triangles. You will only use one of the triangles.

From the dark rose fabric, cut:

■ One 1 3/4" square. Cut the square into half-square triangles.

■ One 3" x 6" strip. Subcut the strip into two 3" squares. Cut the squares into half-square triangles. You will have one triangle left over.

From the floral fabric, cut:

■ One 3" square. Cut the square into half-square triangles. You will have one triangle left over.

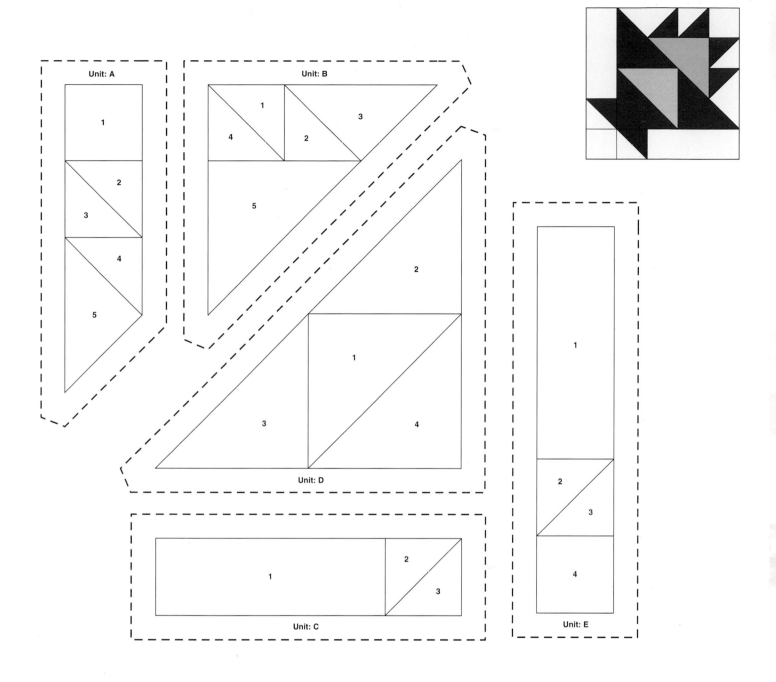

ASSEMBLING THE BLOCK:

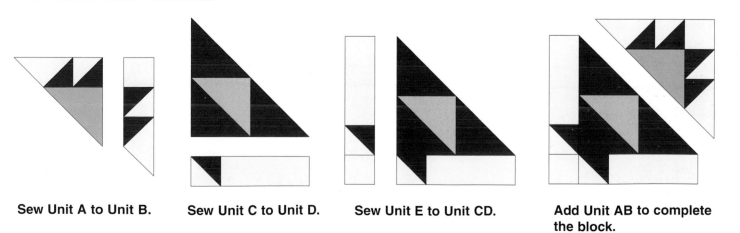

Sew Unit A to Unit B.

Sew Unit C to Unit D.

Sew Unit E to Unit CD.

Add Unit AB to complete the block.

Flower Pot 19.

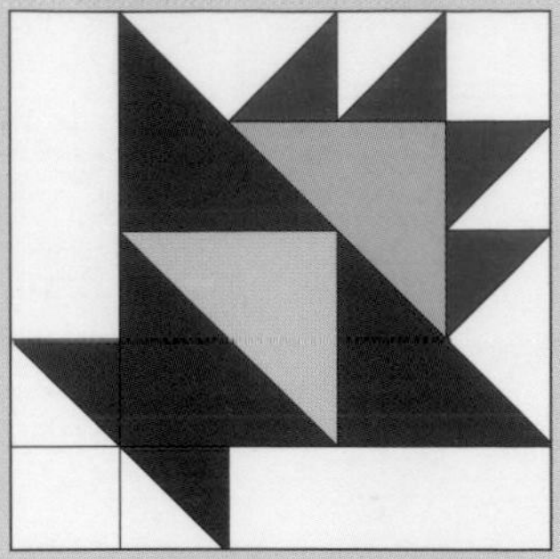

*F*lower *P*ot

January 1937

The Kansas City Star

Position Chart — 4" Block

Fabric	Position #	Size
Unit A – Make 1		
Light	1	1 3/4" x 1 3/4"
Dark Green	2,4	1 3/4" x 1 3/4" ◣
Light	3	1 3/4" x 1 3/4" ◣
Light	5	2 1/2" x 2 1/2" ◣
Unit B – Make 1		
Light	1	1 3/4" x 1 3/4" ◣
Dark Green	2,4	1 3/4" x 1 3/4" ◣
Light	3	2 1/2" x 2 1/2" ◣
Medium	5	3" x 3" ◣
Unit C – Make 1		
Light	1	1 3/4" x 3"
Dark	2	1 3/4" x 1 3/4" ◣
Light	3	1 3/4" x 1 3/4" ◣
Unit D – Make 1		
Floral	1	3" x 3" ◣
Dark	2,3,4	3" x 3" ◣
Unit E – Make 1		
Light	1	1 3/4" x 3"
Dark	2	1 3/4" x 1 3/4" ◣
Light	3	1 3/4" x 1 3/4" ◣
Light	4	1 3/4" x 1 3/4"

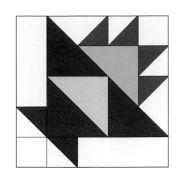

Cutting Directions — Flower Pot 10" Block

From the background fabric, cut:

■ One 3" x 20" strip. Subcut the strip into two 3" squares and two 3" x 7" rectangles.

■ One 3 3/4" x 7 1/2" strip. Subcut the strip into two 3 3/4" squares. Cut the squares into half-square triangles.

■ One 5" square. Cut the square into half-square triangles.

From the green solid fabric, cut:

■ One 3 3/4" x 7 1/2" strip. Subcut the strip into two 3 3/4" squares. Cut the squares into half-square triangles.

From the yellow fabric, cut:

■ One 6" square. Cut the square into half-square triangles. You will only use one of the triangles.

From the rose fabric, cut:

■ One 3 3/4" square. Cut the square into half-square triangles.

■ One 6" x 12" strip. Subcut the strip into two 6" squares. Cut the squares into half-square triangles. You will have one triangle left over.

From the floral fabric, cut:

■ One 6" square. Cut the square into half-square triangles. You will have one triangle left over.

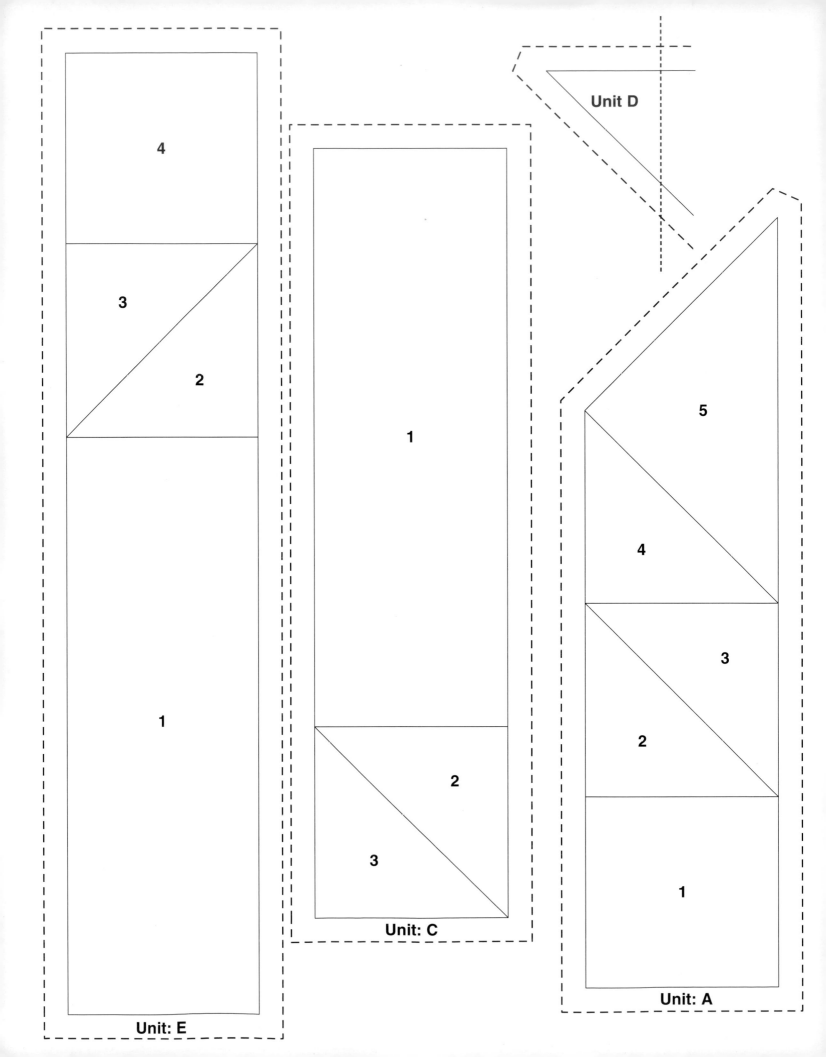

Note: The template for Unit A is too large to fit on the page. Please make a copy of the template and align the dashed lines. Tape the two pieces together to make one complete shape and then stitch your fabric pieces to this foundation.

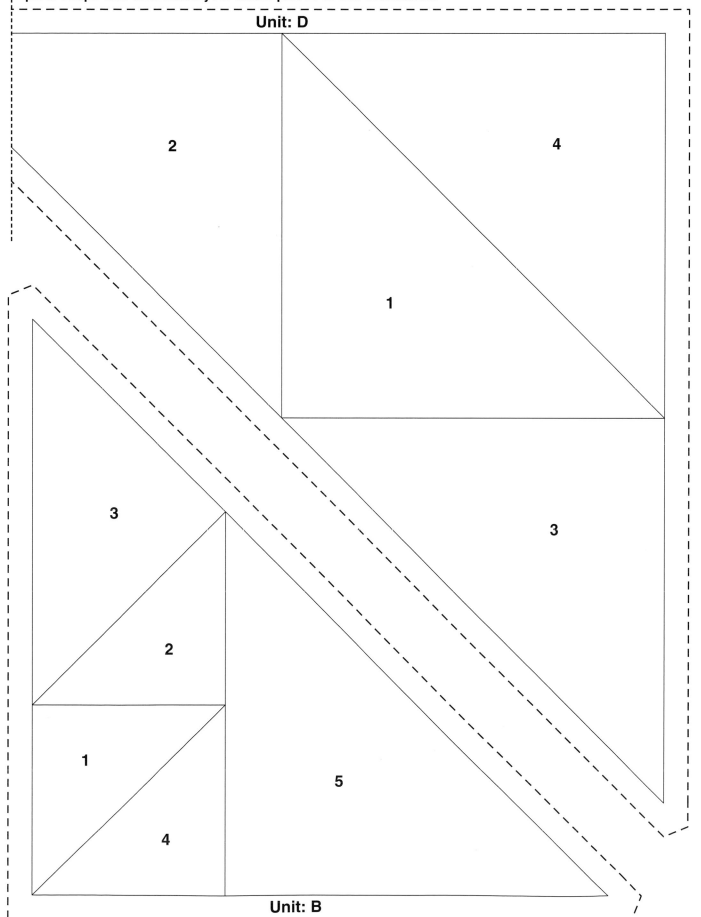

Unit: D

2

4

1

3

3

2

1

5

4

Unit: B

*F*lower *P*ot
January 1937
The Kansas City Star

Position Chart — 10" Block

Fabric	Position #	Size	
Unit A – Make 1			
Background	1	3" x 3"	
Green Solid	2,4	3 3/4" x 3 3/4"	
Background	3	3 3/4" x 3 3/4"	
Background	5	5" x 5"	
Unit B – Make 1			
Background	1	3 3/4" x 3 3/4"	
Green Solid	2,4	3 3/4" x 3 3/4"	
Background	3	5" x 5"	
Yellow Vine	5	6" x 6"	
Unit C – Make 1			
Background	1	3" x 7"	
Rose Solid	2	3 3/4" x 3 3/4"	
Background	3	3 3/4" x 3 3/4"	
Unit D – Make 1			
Floral	1	6" x 6"	
Rose Solid	2,3,4	6" x 6"	
Unit E – Make 1			
Background	1	3" x 7"	
Rose Solid	2	3 3/4" x 3 3/4"	
Background	3	3 3/4" x 3 3/4"	
Background	4	3" x 3"	

When you are ready to sew the units together, refer to the instructions for the 4" block.

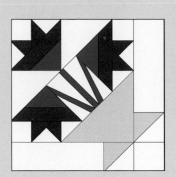

A Basket of *Bright Flowers*

April 1946
The Kansas City Star

Cutting Directions — A Basket of Bright Flowers 4" Block

From the light fabric, cut:

■ One 1 1/4" x 3 3/4" strip. Subcut the strip into three 1 1/4" squares.

■ One 1 1/2" x 4 1/2" strip and subcut the strip into three 1 1/2" squares. Cut the squares into half-square triangles.

■ One 2 1/2" square. Cut the square into two half-square triangles.

■ One strip 1" x 9." Subcut the strip into four 1" x 2 1/4" rectangles.

■ One strip 1 3/4" x 10." Subcut the strip into two 1 3/4" squares and two 1 3/4" x 3 1/4" rectan-

gles. Cut one of the 1 3/4" squares into two half-square triangles.

From the dark rose fabric, cut:

■ One strip 1 1/2" x 4 1/2." Subcut the strip into three 1 1/2" squares. Cut the squares into 6 half-square triangles.

■ One 1" x 9" strip. Cut this strip into three 1" x 3" rectangles.

From the dark green fabric, cut:

■ One 1 3/4" x 3 1/2" strip. Subcut the strip into two

1 3/4" squares. Cut the squares into half-square triangles. You will have one triangle left over.

■ One 1" x 6 3/4" strip. Subcut the strip into three 1" x 2 1/4" rectangles.

From the floral fabric, cut:

■ One 1 3/4" square. Cut the square into two half-square triangles.

■ One 3 1/4" square. Cut the square into two half-square triangles. You will have one triangle left over.

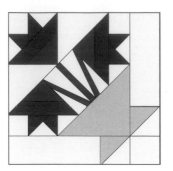

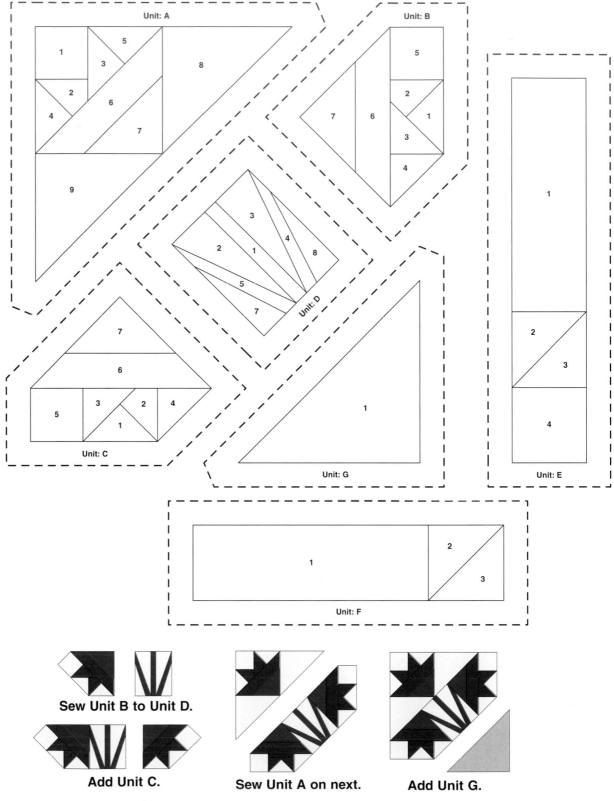

Unit: A

Unit: B

Unit: D

Unit: C

Unit: G

Unit: E

Unit: F

Sew Unit B to Unit D.

Add Unit C.

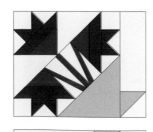

Sew Unit A on next.

Add Unit G.

ASSEMBLING THE BLOCK:

Add Unit F.

Add Unit E to complete the block.

26. A Basket of Bright Flowers

4" Block		
Fabric	**Position #**	**Size**
Unit A – Make 1		
Light	1	1 1/4" x 1/14"
Dark Rose	2,3	1 1/2" x 1 1/2"
Light	4,5	1 1/2" x 1 1/2"
Dark Rose	6	1" x 3"
Dark Green	7	1 3/4" x 1 3/4"
Light	8,9	2 1/2" x 2 1/2"
Unit B – Make 1		
Light	1	1 1/2" x 1 1/2"
Dark Rose	2,3	1 1/2" x 1 1/2"
Light	4	1 1/2" x 1 1/2"
Light	5	1 1/4" x 1 1/4"
Dark Rose	6	1" x 3"
Dark Green	7	1 3/4" x 1 3/4"
Unit C – Make 1		
Light	1	1 1/2" x 1 1/2"
Dark Rose	2,3	1 1/2" x 1 1/2"
Light	4	1 1/2" x 1 1/2"
Light	5	1 1/4" x 1 1/4"
Dark Rose	6	1" x 3"
Dark Green	7	1 3/4" x 1 3/4"
Unit D – Make 1		
Dark Green	1,4,5	1" x 2 1/4"
Light	2,3,6,7	1" x 2 1/4"
Unit E – Make 1		
Light	1	1 3/4" x 3 1/4"
Floral	2	1 3/4" x 1 3/4"
Light	3	1 3/4" x 1 3/4"
Light	4	1 3/4" x 1 3/4"
Unit F - Make 1		
Light	1	1 3/4" x 3 1/4"
Floral	2	1 3/4" x 1 3/4"
Light	3	1 3/4" x 1 3/4"
Unit G - Make 1		
Floral	1	3 1/4" x 3 1/4"

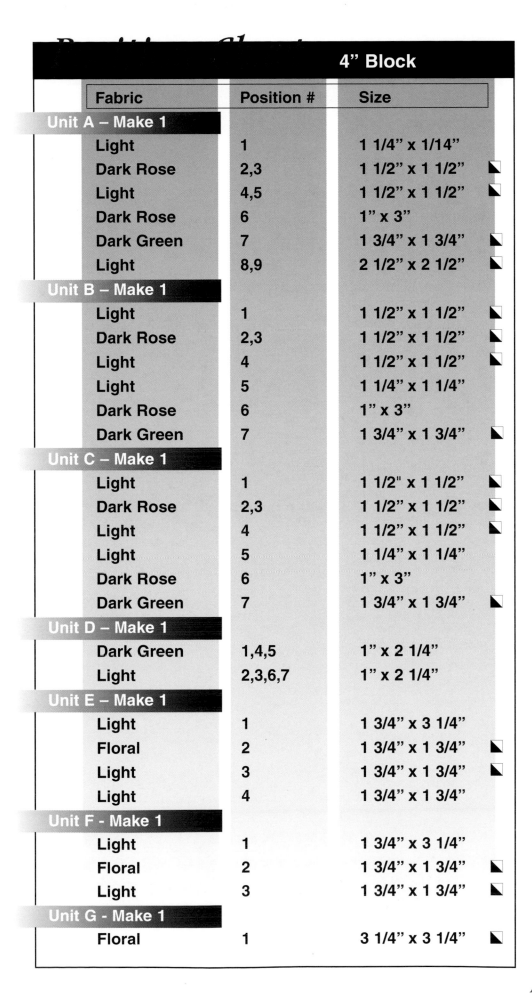

*A B*asket of *B*right *F*lowers
April 1946
The Kansas City Star

Cutting Directions — A Basket of Bright Flowers 10" Block

From the background fabric, cut:

■ One strip 2 1/4" x 6 3/4." Subcut the strip into three 2 1/4" squares.

■ One 2 3/4" x 8 1/4" strip. Subcut the strip into three 2 3/4" squares. Cut the squares into half-square triangles.

■ One 4 3/4" square. Cut the square into half-square triangles.

■ One 2" x 17" strip. Subcut the strip into four 2" x 4 1/4" rectangles.

■ One 3 1/2" square. Cut the square into half-square triangles.

■ One 3" x 17" strip. Subcut the strip into one 3" square and two 3" x 7" rectangles.

From the solid rose fabric, cut:

■ One 2 3/4" x 8 1/4" strip. Subcut the strip into three 2 3/4" squares. Cut the squares into half-square triangles.

From the rose fabric, cut:

■ One 1 3/4" x 18" strip. Subcut the strip into three 1 3/4" x 6" rectangles.

From the solid green fabric, cut:

■ One 3 1/2" x 7" strip. Subcut the strip into two

3 1/2" squares. Cut the two squares into half-square triangles. You will have one triangle left over.

■ One 1 1/4" x 13 1/2" strip. Subcut the strip into three 1 1/4" x 4 1/2" rectangles.

From the green vine fabric, cut:

■ One 3 1/2" square. Subcut the square into half-square triangles.

■ One 6 1/2" square. Subcut the square into half-square triangles. You will have one triangle left over.

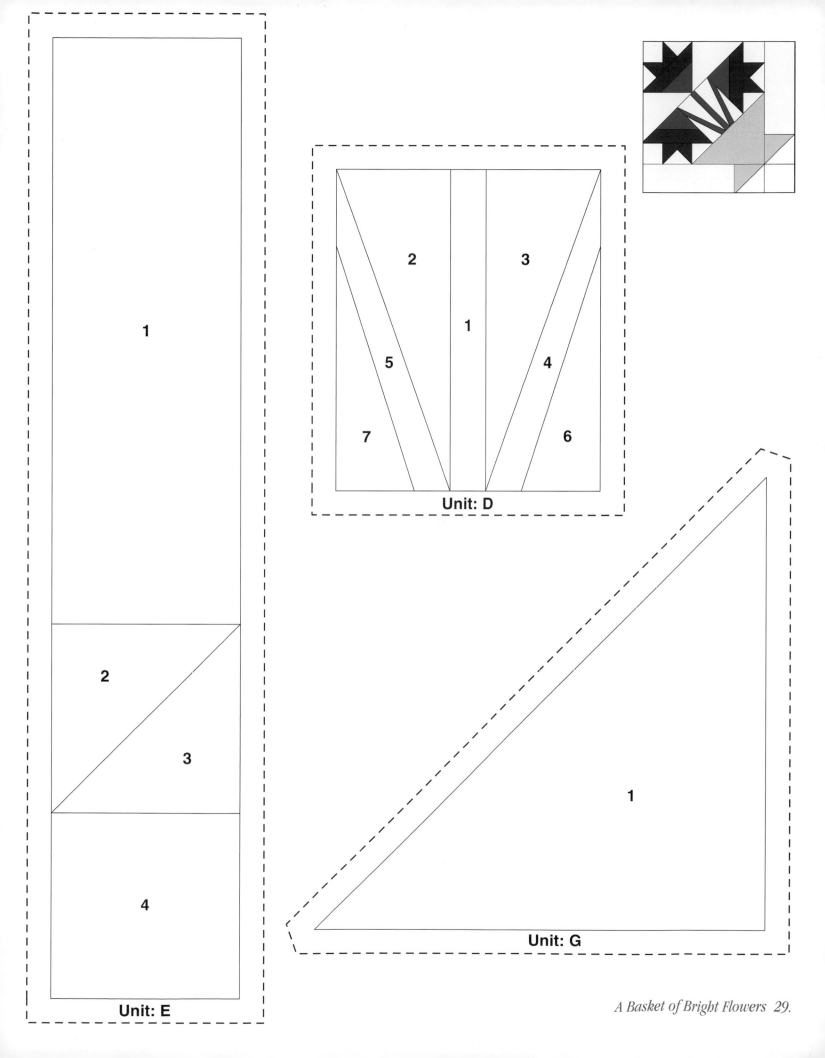

Unit: E

Unit: D

Unit: G

A Basket of Bright Flowers 29.

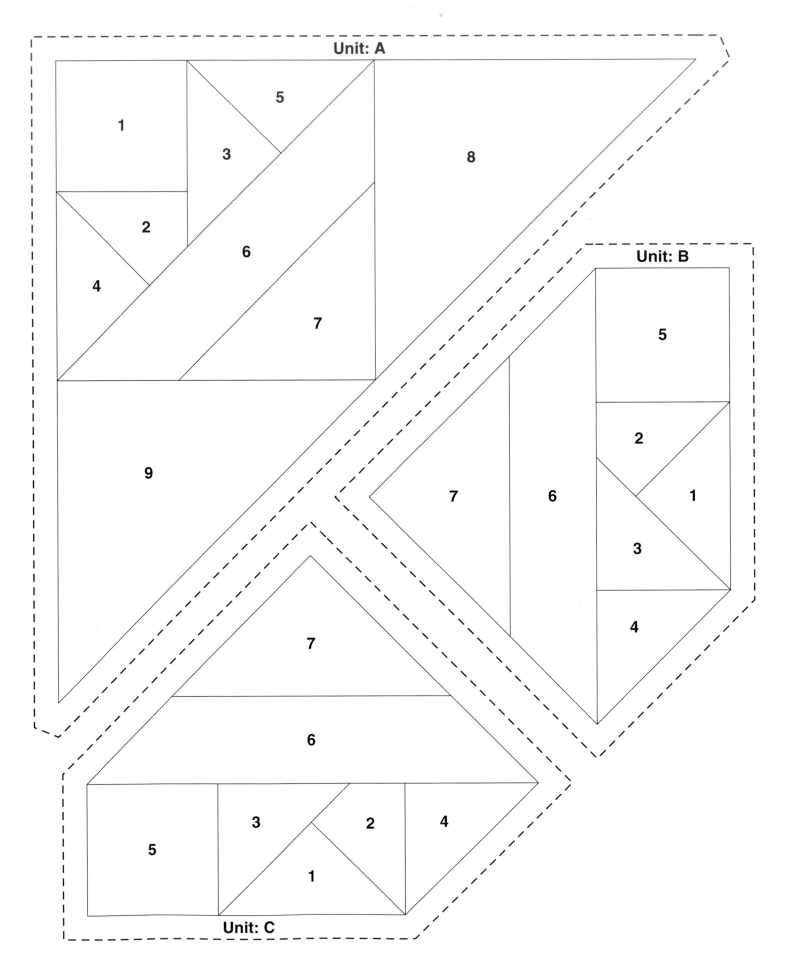

Unit: A

Unit: B

Unit: C

30. A Basket of Bright Flowers

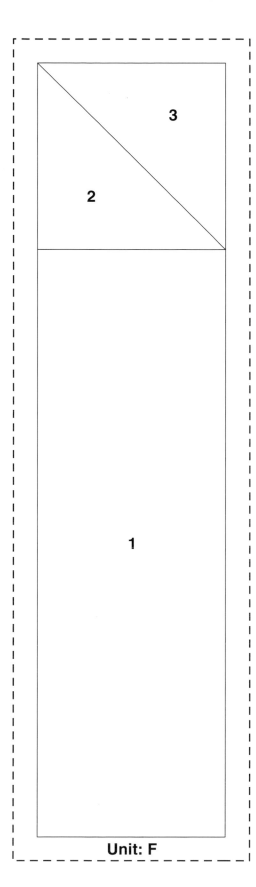

Unit: F

Sew the units together as shown in the instructions for the 4" block.

Fabric	Position #	Size	
Unit A – Make 1			
Background	1	2 1/4" x 2 1/4"	
Rose Solid	2,3	2 3/4" x 2 3/4"	
Background	4,5	2 3/4" x 2 3/4"	
Rose	6	1 3/4" x 6"	
Green Solid	7	3 1/2" x 3 1/2"	
Background	8,9	4 3/4" x 4 3/4"	
Unit B – Make 1			
Background	1	2 3/4" x 2 3/4"	
Rose Solid	2,3	2 3/4" x 2 3/4"	
Background	4	2 3/4" x 2 3/4"	
Background	5	2 1/4" x 2 1/4"	
Rose	6	1 3/4" x 6"	
Green Solid	7	3 1/2" x 3 1/2"	
Unit C – Make 1			
Background	1	2 3/4" x 2 3/4"	
Rose Solid	2,3	2 3/4" x 2 3/4"	
Background	4	2 3/4" x 2 3/4"	
Background	5	2 1/4" x 2 1/4"	
Rose	6	1 3/4" x 6"	
Green Solid	7	3 1/2" x 3 1/2"	
Unit D – Make 1			
Green Solid	1,4,5	1 1/4" x 4 1/2"	
Background	2,3,6,7	2" x 4 1/4"	
Unit E – Make 1			
Background	1	3" x 7"	
Green Vine	2	3 1/2" x 3 1/2"	
Background	3	3 1/2" x 3 1/2"	
Background	4	3" x 3"	
Unit F - Make 1			
Background	1	3" x 7"	
Green Vine	2	3 1/2" x 3 1/2"	
Background	3	3 1/2" x 3 1/2"	
Unit G - Make 1			
Green Vine	1	6 1/2" x 6 1/2"	

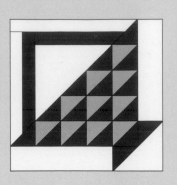

Cherry Basket
October 1928
The Kansas City Star

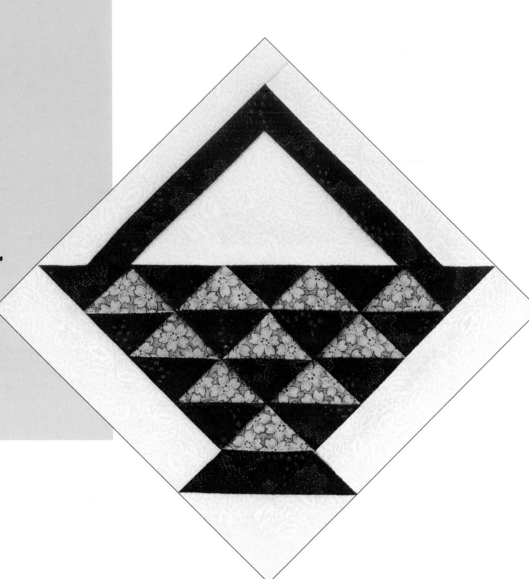

Cutting Directions — Cherry Basket 4" Block

From the light fabric, cut:

■ One 3 1/4" square. Cut the square into half-square triangles.

■ One 1" x 9" strip. Subcut the strip into two 1" x 4 1/2" rectangles.

■ One 1 1/4" x 7" strip. Subcut the strip into two 1 1/4" x 3 1/2" rectangles.

From the dark fabric, cut:

■ One 1" x 7" strip. Subcut the strip into two 1" x 3 1/2" rectangles.

■ One 1 3/4" x 15 3/4" strip. Subcut the strip into nine 1 3/4" squares. Cut the squares into half-square triangles. You will have one triangle left over.

From the medium fabric, cut:

■ One 1 3/4" x 8 3/4" strip. Subcut the strip into five 1 3/4" squares. Cut the squares into half-square triangles.

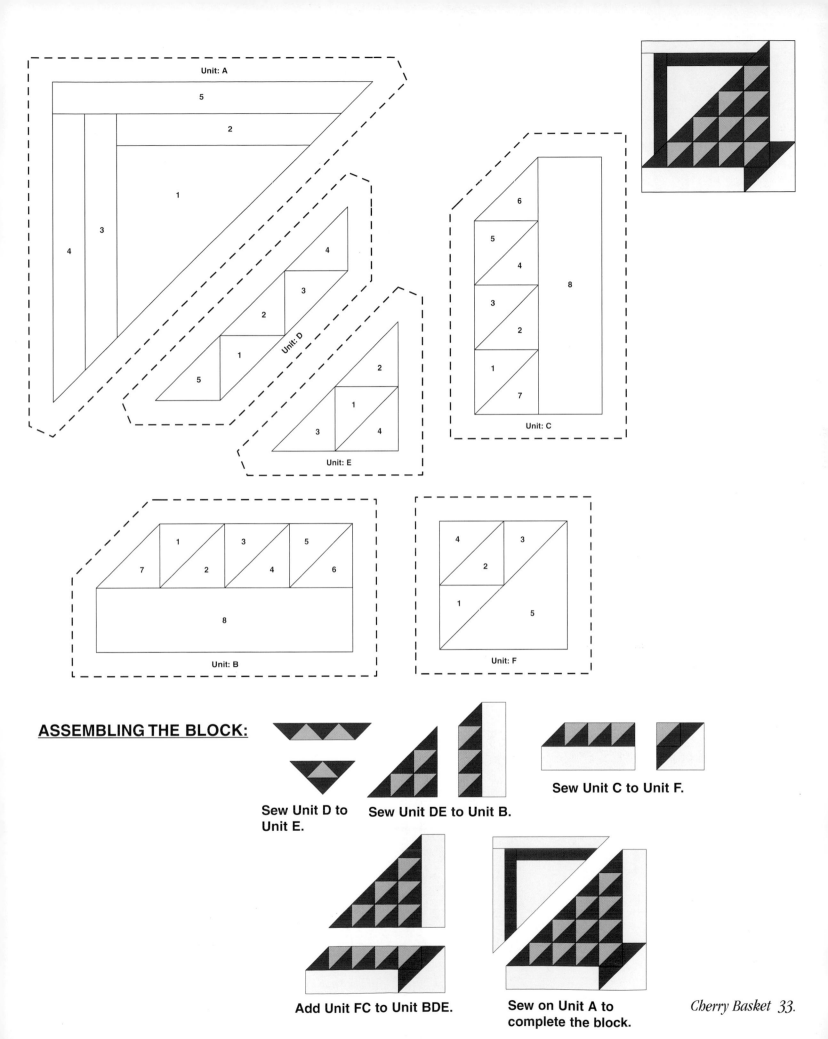

Unit: A

5

2

1

3

4

Unit: D

4

3

2

1

5

Unit: E

2

1

3

4

Unit: C

6

5

4

3

2

1

7

8

Unit: B

1

3

5

7

2

4

6

8

Unit: F

4

3

2

1

5

ASSEMBLING THE BLOCK:

Sew Unit D to
Unit E.

Sew Unit DE to Unit B.

Sew Unit C to Unit F.

Add Unit FC to Unit BDE.

Sew on Unit A to
complete the block.

Cherry Basket 33.

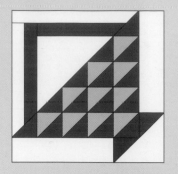

Position Chart — 4" Block

Fabric	Position #	Size
Unit A – Make 1		
Light	1	3 1/4" x 3 1/4"
Dark	2,3	1" x 3 1/2"
Light	4,5	1" x 4 1/2"
Unit B – Make 1		
Medium	1,3,5	1 3/4" x 1 3/4"
Dark	2,4,6,7	1 3/4" x 1 3/4"
Light	8	1 1/4" x 3 1/2"
Unit C – Make 1		
Medium	1,3,5	1 3/4" x 1 3/4"
Dark	2,4,6,7	1 3/4" x 1 3/4"
Light	8	1 1/4" x 3 1/2"
Unit D – Make 1		
Medium	1,3	1 3/4" x 1 3/4"
Dark	2,4,5	1 3/4" x 1 3/4"
Unit E – Make 1		
Medium	1	1 3/4" x 1 3/4"
Dark	2,3,4	1 3/4" x 1 3/4"
Unit F – Make 1		
Dark	1,2,3	1 3/4" x 1 3/4"
Medium	4	1 3/4" x 1 3/4"
Light	5	3 1/4" x 3 1/4"

This wall hanging was made by Debbie Dent of Bozeman, Montana, using the Cherry Basket, Flower Pot and May Basket in Floral Tones block patterns given in this book.

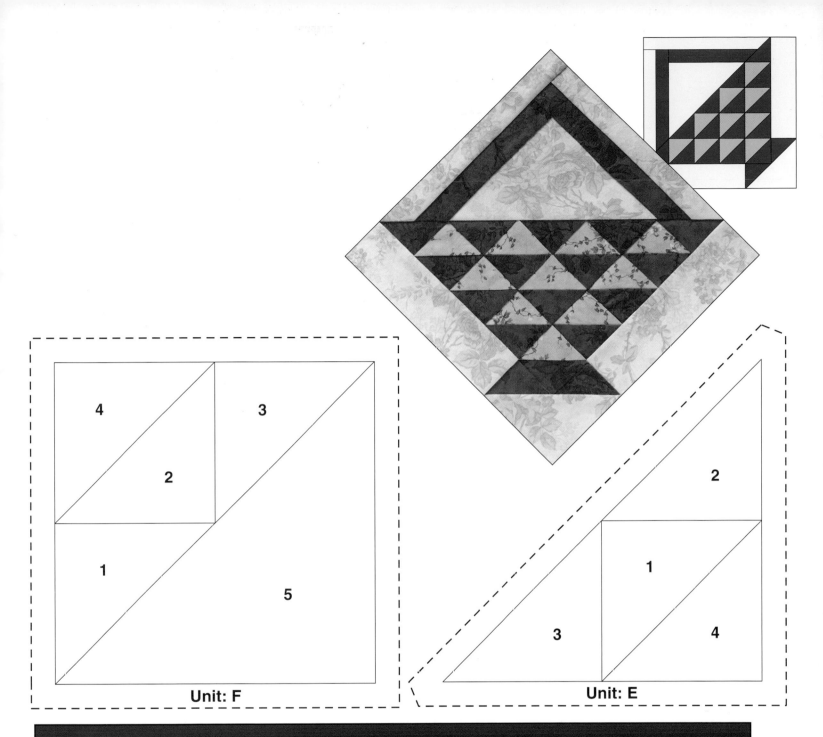

Unit: F

Unit: E

Cutting Directions — Cherry Basket 10" Block

From the background fabric, cut:

■ One 7" square. Cut the square into half-square triangles. Subcut one half-square triangle in half again.

■ One 1 3/4" x 18 1/2" strip. Subcut the strip into two 1 3/4" x 9 1/4" rectangles.

■ One 2 1/2" x 15 1/2" strip. Subcut the strip into two 2 1/2" x 7 3/4" rectangles.

From the rose fabric, cut:

■ One 1 1/2" x 15" strip. Subcut the strip into two 1 1/2" x 7 1/2" rectangles.

■ One 3 1/4" x 29 1/4" strip. Subcut the strip into nine 3 1/4"

squares. Cut the squares into half-square triangles. You will have one triangle left over.

From the yellow vine fabric, cut:

■ One 3 1/4" x 16 1/4" strip. Subcut the strip into five 3 1/4" squares. Cut the squares into half-square triangles.

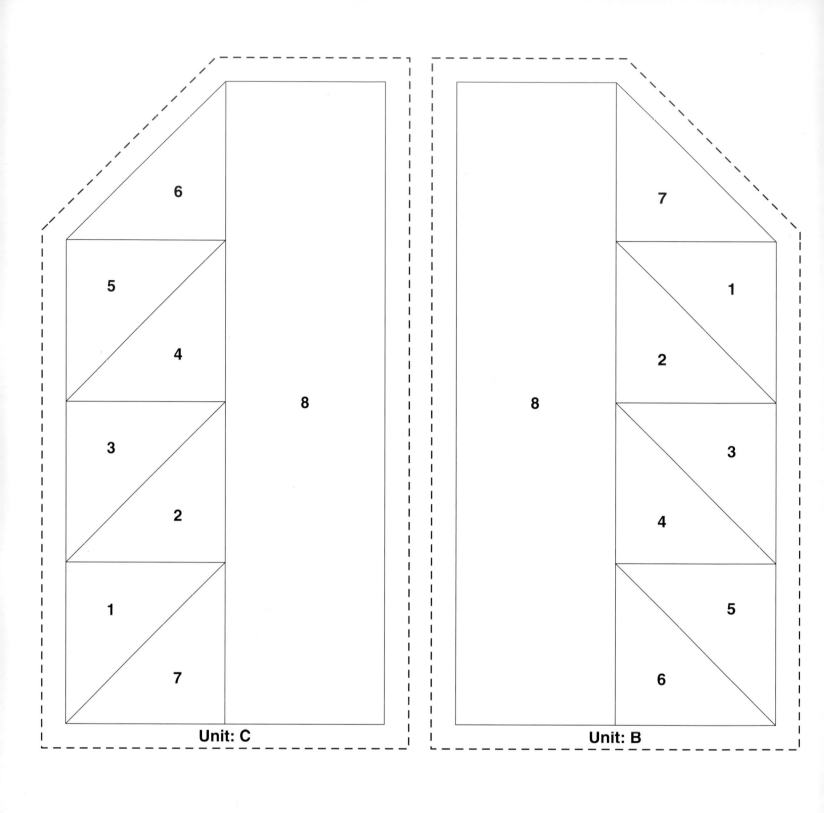

Unit: C

Unit: B

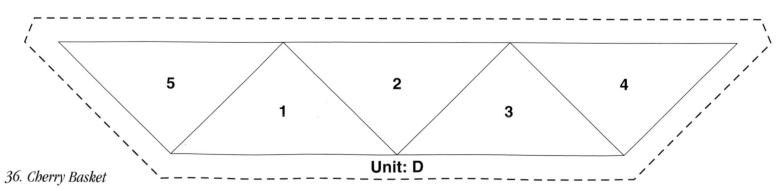

Unit: D

36. Cherry Basket

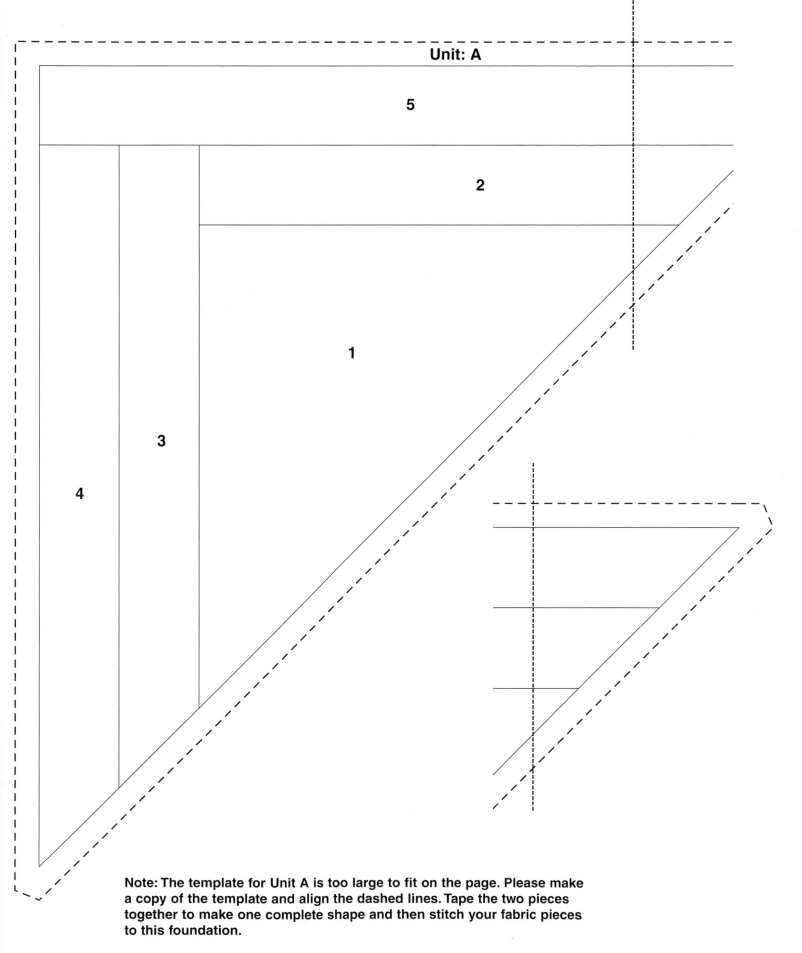

Unit: A

5

2

1

3

4

Note: The template for Unit A is too large to fit on the page. Please make a copy of the template and align the dashed lines. Tape the two pieces together to make one complete shape and then stitch your fabric pieces to this foundation.

Cherry Basket
October 1928
The Kansas City Star

Position Chart

Position Chart — 10" Block

Fabric	Position #	Size	
Unit A – Make 1			
Background	1	7" x 7"	
Rose	2,3	1 1/2" x 7 1/2"	
Background	4,5	1 3/4" x 9 1/4"	
Unit B – Make 1			
Yellow Vine	1,3,5	3 1/4" x 3 1/4"	
Rose	2,4,6,7	3 1/4" x 3 1/4"	
Background	8	2 1/2" x 7 3/4"	
Unit C – Make 1			
Yellow Vine	1,3,5	3 1/4" x 3 1/4"	
Rose	2,4,6,7	3 1/4" x 3 1/4"	
Background	8	2 1/2" x 7 3/4"	
Unit D – Make 1			
Yellow Vine	1,3	3 1/4" x 3 1/4"	
Rose	2,4,5	3 1/4" x 3 1/4"	
Unit E – Make 1			
Yellow Vine	1	3 1/4" x 3 1/4"	
Rose	2,3,4	3 1/4" x 3 1/4"	
Unit F – Make 1			
Rose	1,2,3	3 1/4" x 3 1/4"	
Yellow Vine	4	3 1/4" x 3 1/4"	
Background	5	5" x 5"	

When you are ready to put the units together, refer to the directions for the 4" block.

Historic Oak Leaf
January 1961
The Kansas City Star

Cutting Directions — The Historic Oak Leaf 4" Block

From the floral fabric, cut:

■ One 1 3/4" x 8 3/4" strip Subcut the strip into five 1 3/4" squares. Cut the squares into half-square triangles. You will have one left over.

■ One 3" x 6" strip. Cut the strip into two 3" squares. Cut the squares into half-square triangles.

From the dark green fabric, cut:

■ One 1 3/4" x 10 1/2" strip. Subcut the strip into six 1 3/4" squares. Cut the squares into half-square triangles. You will have one left over.

■ One 2 1/4" x 4 1/2" strip. Subcut the strip into two 2 1/4" squares. Cut one of the squares into half-square triangles.

■ One 1 1/4" x 3 3/4" strip.

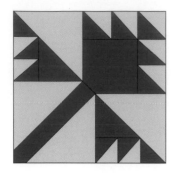

Historic
Oak **L**eaf
January 1961
The Kansas City Star

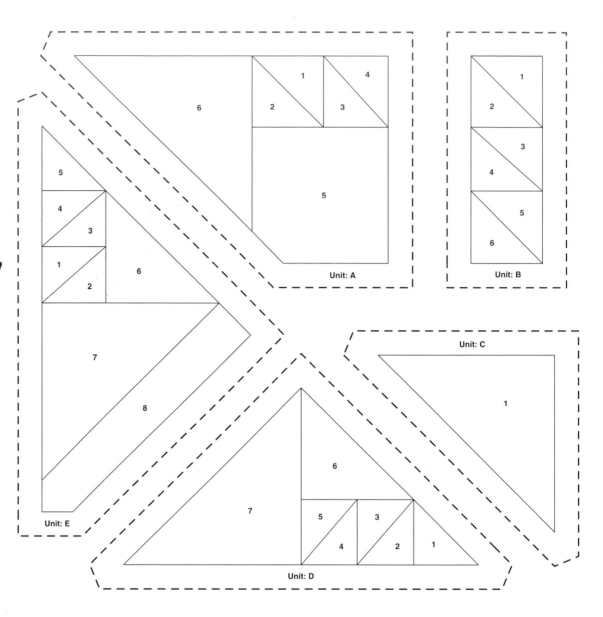

Unit: A

Unit: B

Unit: C

Unit: D

Unit: E

ASSEMBLING THE BLOCK:

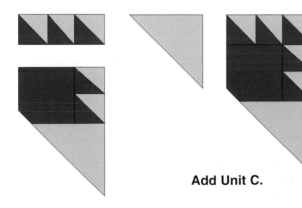

Sew Unit A to Unit B.

Add Unit C.

Sew Unit D to Unit E.

Sew the two halves together to complete the block.

Fabric	Position #	Size	
Unit A – Make 1			
Floral	1,4	1 3/4" x 1 3/4"	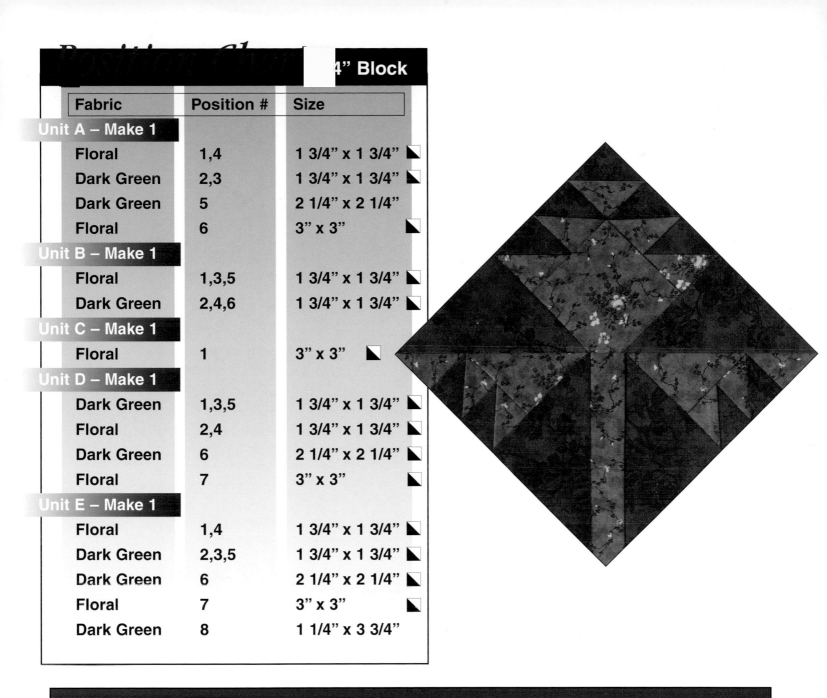
Dark Green	2,3	1 3/4" x 1 3/4"	
Dark Green	5	2 1/4" x 2 1/4"	
Floral	6	3" x 3"	
Unit B – Make 1			
Floral	1,3,5	1 3/4" x 1 3/4"	
Dark Green	2,4,6	1 3/4" x 1 3/4"	
Unit C – Make 1			
Floral	1	3" x 3"	
Unit D – Make 1			
Dark Green	1,3,5	1 3/4" x 1 3/4"	
Floral	2,4	1 3/4" x 1 3/4"	
Dark Green	6	2 1/4" x 2 1/4"	
Floral	7	3" x 3"	
Unit E – Make 1			
Floral	1,4	1 3/4" x 1 3/4"	
Dark Green	2,3,5	1 3/4" x 1 3/4"	
Dark Green	6	2 1/4" x 2 1/4"	
Floral	7	3" x 3"	
Dark Green	8	1 1/4" x 3 3/4"	

Cutting Directions — The Historic Oak Leaf 10" Block

From the rose fabric, cut:

■ One 3 1/4" x 16 1/4" strip. Subcut the strip into five 3 1/4" squares. Cut the squares into half-square triangles. You will have one triangle left over.

■ One 6 1/4" x 12 1/2" strip. Subcut the strip into two 6 1/4" squares. Cut the squares into half-square triangles.

From the green fabric, cut:

■ One 3 1/4" x 19 1/2" strip. Subcut the strip into six 3 1/4" squares. Cut the squares into half-square triangles. You will have one triangle left over.

■ One 4 1/2" x 9" strip. Subcut the strip into two 4 1/2" squares. Cut one of the squares into half-square triangles.

■ One 2" x 8 1/4" strip.

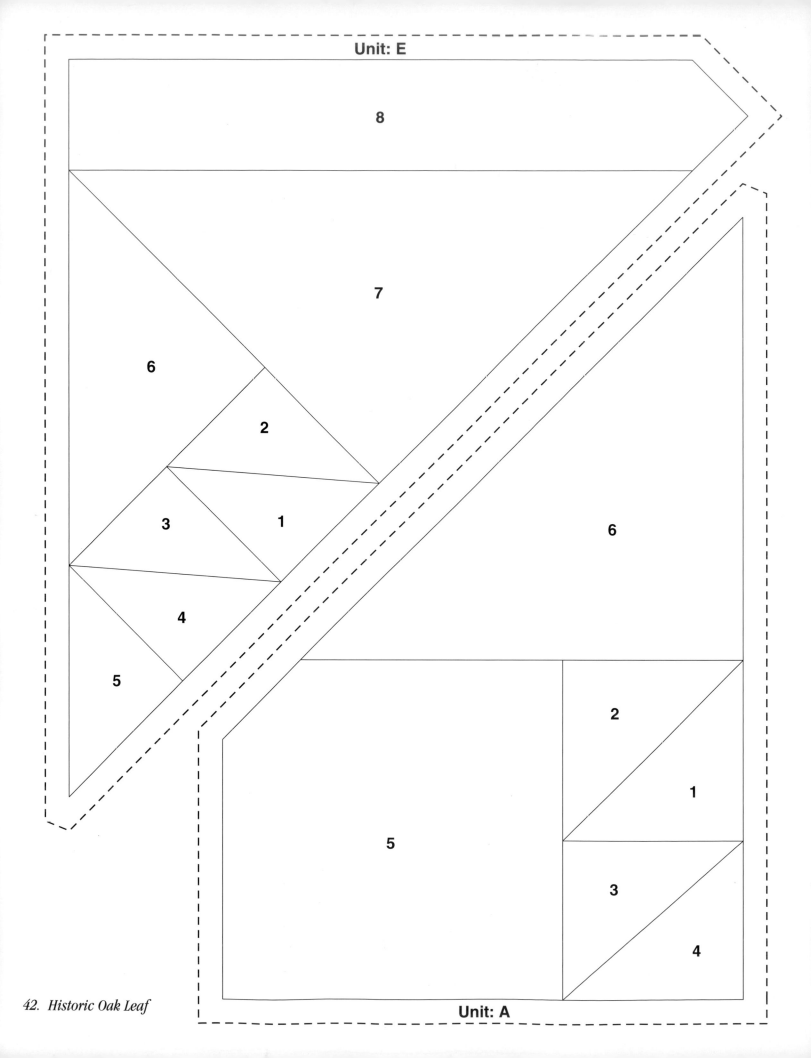

Unit: E

8

7

6

2

3

1

4

5

6

2

1

5

3

4

Unit: A

42. *Historic Oak Leaf*

Unit: D

6

1

3

2

5

4

7

1

Unit: C

1

3

5

2

4

6

Unit: B

Historic Oak Leaf

January 1961

The Kansas City Star

Position Chart — 10" Block

Fabric	Position #	Size	
Unit A – Make 1			
Rose	1,4	3 1/4" x 3 1/4"	
Green Vine	2,3	3 1/4" x 3 1/4"	
Green Vine	5	4 1/2" x 4 1/2"	
Rose	6	6 1/4" x 6 1/4"	
Unit B – Make 1			
Rose	1,3,5	3 1/4" x 3 1/4"	
Green Vine	2,4,6	3 1/4" x 3 1/4"	
Unit C – Make 1			
Rose	1	6 1/4" x 6 1/4"	
Unit D – Make 1			
Green Vine	1,3,5	3 1/4" x 3 1/4"	
Rose	2,4	3 1/4" x 3 1/4"	
Green Vine	6	4 1/2" x 4 1/2"	
Rose	7	6 1/4" x 6 1/4"	
Unit E – Make 1			
Rose	1,4	3 1/4" x 3 1/4"	
Green Vine	2,3,5	3 1/4" x 3 1/4"	
Green Vine	6	4 1/2" x 4 1/2"	
Rose	7	6 1/4" x 6 1/4"	
Green Vine	8	2" x 8 1/4"	

To sew the units together, refer to the instructions for the 4" block.

Garden Maze

May 1932
The Kansas City Star

From the light fabric, cut:

■ One 2 1/4" square.

■ One 1" x 9" strip. Subcut the strip into four 1" X 2 1/4" rectangles.

■ One 1 1/2" x 12" strip. Subcut the strip into eight 1 1/2" squares. Cut the squares into half-square triangles.

From the dark green fabric, cut:

■ One 1" x 9" strip. Subcut the strip into four 1" x 2 1/4" rectangles.

■ One 1" x 6" strip. Subcut the strip into four 1" x 1 1/2" rectangles.

■ One 1 1/4" x 6" strip. Subcut the strip into two 1 1/4" x 3" rectangles.

From the floral fabric, cut:

■ One 1" x 9" strip. Subcut the strip into four 1" x 2 1/4" rectangles.

■ One 1" x 6" strip. Subcut the strip into four 1" x 1 1/2" rectangles.

■ One 1 1/4" x 6" strip. Subcut the strip into two 1 1/4" x 3" rectangles.

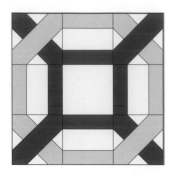

Garden Maze

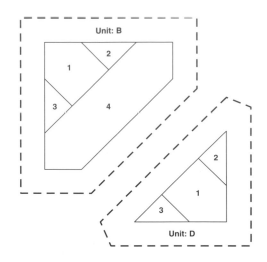

Unit: B

Unit: D

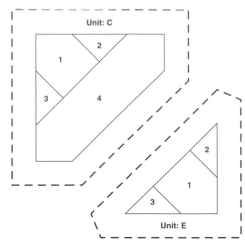

Unit: C

Unit: E

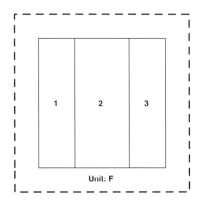

Unit: F

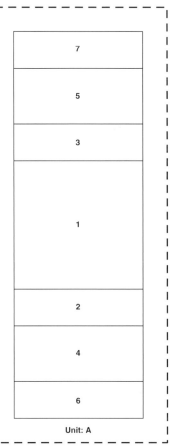

Unit: A

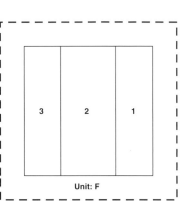

Unit: F

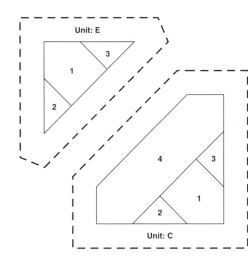

Unit: E

Unit: C

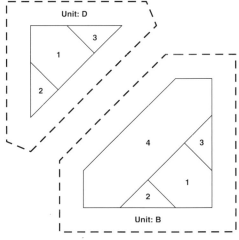

Unit: D

Unit: B

ASSEMBLING THE BLOCK:

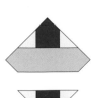

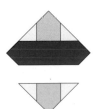

Sew each Unit B to a Unit D as shown.

Sew each Unit E to a Unit C.

Sew Unit F to Unit BD.

Then add the Unit CE. Make two of these.

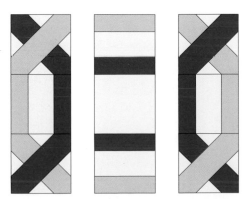

Add Units BCDEF to Unit A to complete the block.

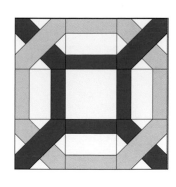

Position Chart — 4" Block

Fabric	Position #	Size
Unit A – Make 1		
Light	1	2 1/4" x 2 1/4"
Dark Green	2,3	1" x 2 1/4"
Light	4,5	1" x 2 1/4"
Floral	6,7	1" x 2 1/4"
Unit B – Make 2		
Dark Green	1	1" x 1 1/2"
Light	2,3	1 1/2" x 1 1/2"
Floral	4	1 1/4" x 3"
Unit C – Make 2		
Floral	1	1" x 1 1/2"
Light	2,3	1 1/2" x 1 1/2"
Dark Green	4	1 1/4" x 3"
Unit D – Make 2		
Dark Green	1	1" x 1 1/2"
Light	2,3	1 1/2" x 1 1/2"
Unit E – Make 2		
Floral	1	1" x 1 1/2"
Light	2,3	1 1/2" x 1 1/2"
Unit F – Make 2		
Floral	1	1" x 2 1/4"
Light	2	1" x 2 1/4"
Dark Green	3	1" x 2 1/4"

Garden Maze

May 1932
The Kansas City Star

1	
2	
3	

Unit: F *(Make 2)*

Cutting Directions — Garden Maze 10" Block

From the background fabric, cut:

■ One 4 1/4" square.

■ One 2 1/4" x 17" strip. Subcut the strip into four 2 1/4" X 4 1/4" rectangles.

■ One 2 1/2" x 20" strip. Subcut the strip into eight 2 1/2" squares. Cut the squares into half-square triangles.

From the green fabric, cut:

■ One 1 3/4" x 17" strip. Subcut the strip into four 1 3/4" x 4 1/4" rectangles.

■ One 2 1/2" x 11" strip. Subcut the strip into four 2 1/2" x 2 3/4" rectangles.

■ One 2" x 11 1/2" strip. Subcut the strip into two 2" x 5 3/4" rectangles.

From the rose fabric, cut:

■ One 1 3/4" x 17" strip. Subcut the strip into four 1 3/4" x 4 1/4" rectangles.

■ One 2 1/2" x 11" strip. Subcut the strip into four 2 1/2" x 2 3/4" rectangles.

■ One 2" x 11 1/2" strip. Subcut the strip into two 2" x 5 3/4" rectangles.

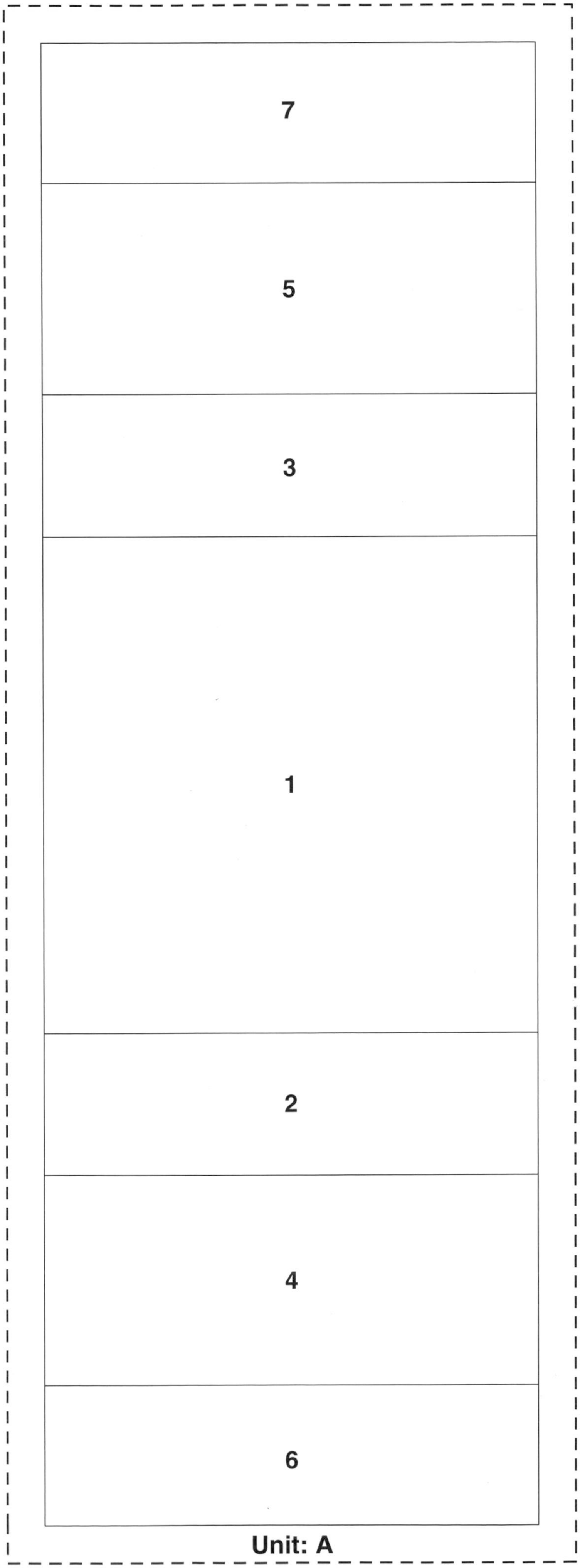

7

5

3

1

2

4

6

Unit: A

Unit: E *(Make 2)*

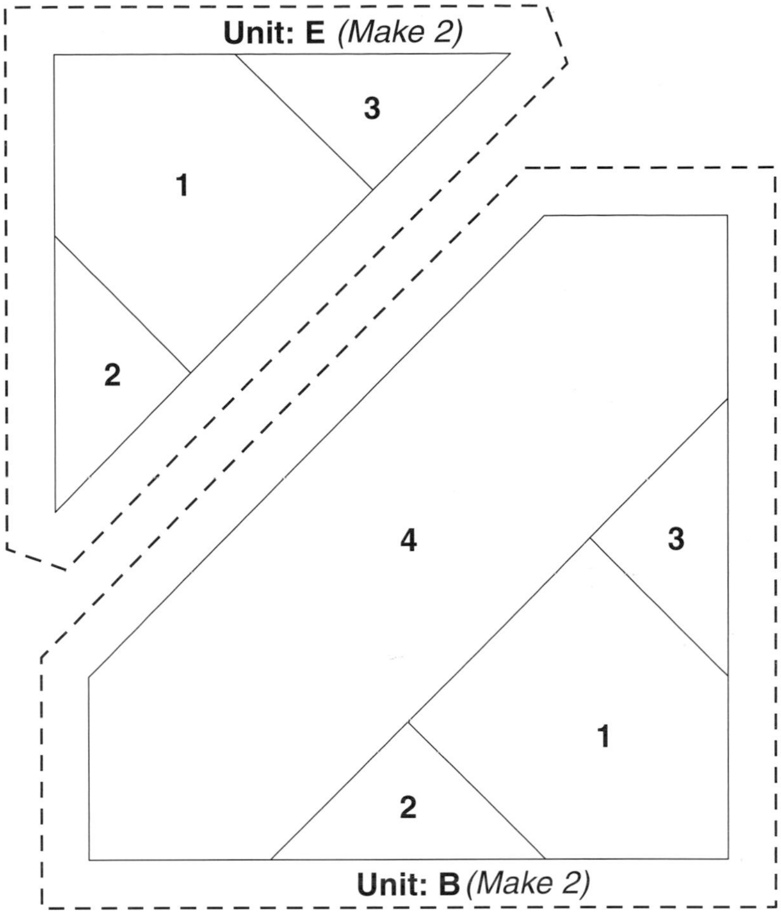

3

1

2

4

3

1

2

Unit: B *(Make 2)*

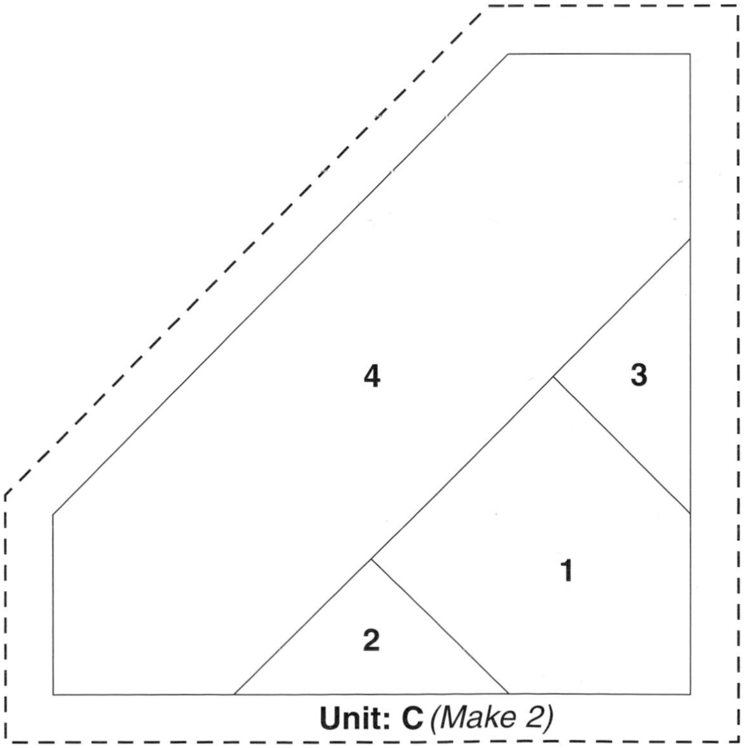

4

3

1

2

Unit: C *(Make 2)*

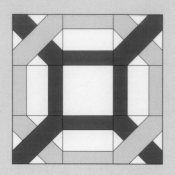

Garden Maze
May 1932
The Kansas City Star

Fabric	Position #	Size	10" Block
Unit A – Make 1			
Background	1	4 1/4" x 4 1/4"	
Green Vine	2,3	1 3/4" x 4 1/4"	
Background	4,5	2 1/4" x 4 1/4"	
Rose	6,7	1 3/4" x 4 1/4"	
Unit B – Make 2			
Green Vine	1	2 1/2 " x 2 3/4"	
Background	2,3	2 1/2" x 2 1/2"	◥
Rose	4	2" x 5 3/4"	
Unit C – Make 2			
Rose	1	2 1/2" x 2 3/4"	
Background	2,3	2 1/2" x 2 1/2"	◥
Green Vine	4	2" x 5 3/4"	
Unit D – Make 2			
Green Vine	1	2 1/2" x 2 3/4"	
Background	2,3	2 1/2" x 2 1/2"	◥
Unit E – Make 2			
Rose	1	2 1/2" x 2 3/4"	
Background	2,3	2 1/2" x 2 1/2"	◥
Unit F – Make 2			
Rose	1	1 3/4" x 4 1/4"	
Background	2	2 1/4" x 4 1/4"	
Green Vine	3	1 3/4" x 4 1/4"	

When you are ready to sew the units together, refer to the directions for the 4" block.

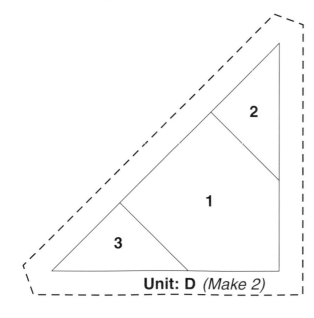

Unit: D *(Make 2)*

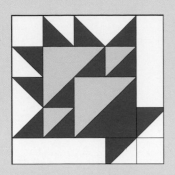

May Basket in Floral Tones
September 1947
The Kansas City Star

From the light fabric, cut:

■ One 2" x 8" strip. Subcut the strip into four 2" squares. Cut two of the squares into half-square triangles.

■ One 2 1/4" square. Subcut the square into two half-square triangles.

■ One 1 1/2" x 6" strip. Subcut the strip into two 1 1/2" x 3" rectangles.

From the floral fabric, cut:

■ One 2" square. Subcut the square into 2 half-square triangles.

■ One 2 3/4" square. Subcut into 2 half-square triangles.

From the dark green fabric, cut:

■ One strip 2" x 12." Subcut the strip into 6 squares. Cut the squares into half-square triangles.

■ One 2 3/4" square. Subcut the square into 2 half-square triangles. You will have one half-square triangle left over.

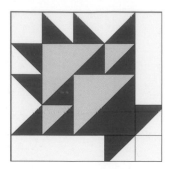

May Basket in Floral Tones
September 1947
The Kansas City Star

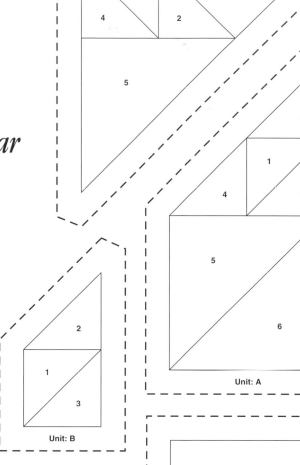

Unit: C

Unit: A

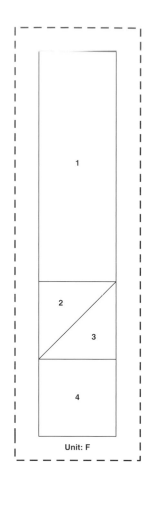

Unit: F

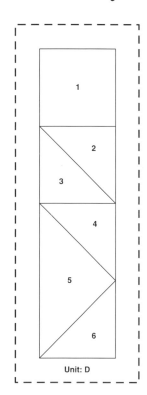

Unit: D

Unit: B

Unit: E

ASSEMBLING THE BLOCK:

Sew Unit A to Unit B.

Add Unit C as shown.

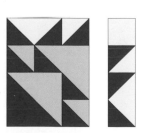

Next add Unit D.

Unit E is the next one to be added.

Sew on Unit F as shown to complete the block.

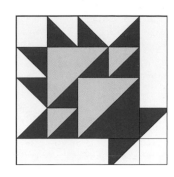

Position chart	4" Block	
Fabric	**Position #**	**Size**
Unit A – Make 1		
Floral	1	2" x 2"
Dark Green	2,3,4	2" x 2"
Floral	5	2 3/4" x 2 3/4"
Dark Green	6	2 3/4" x 2 3/4"
Unit B – Make 1		
Floral	1	2" x 2"
Dark Green	2,3	2" x 2"
Unit C – Make 1		
Light	1	2" x 2"
Dark Green	2,4	2" x 2"
Light	3	2 1/4" x 2 1/4"
Floral	5	2 3/4" x 2 3/4"
Unit D – Make 1		
Light	1	2" x 2"
Dark Green	2,4,6	2" x 2"
Light	3	2" x 2"
Light	5	2 1/4" x 2 1/4"
Unit E – Make 1		
Light	1	1 1/2" x 3"
Dark Green	2	2" x 2"
Light	3	2" x 2"
Unit F – Make 1		
Light	1	1 1/2" x 3"
Dark Green	2	2" x 2"
Light	3	2" x 2"
Light	4	2" x 2"

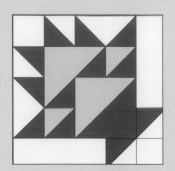

May Basket in Floral Tones
September 1947
The Kansas City Star

From the background fabric, cut:

■ One 3 1/2" x 7" strip. Subcut the strip into two 3 1/2" squares. Cut the squares into half-square triangles.

■ Two 3" squares.

■ One 4 3/4" square. Cut the square into half-square triangles.

■ One 3" x 13 1/2" strip. Subcut the strip into two 3" x 6 3/4" rectangles.

From the floral fabric, cut:

■ One 3 1/2" square. Subcut the square into two half-square triangles.

■ One 5 1/2" square. Subcut the square into two half-square triangles.

From the green fabric, cut:

■ One 3 1/2" x 21" strip. Subcut the strip into 6 squares. Cut the squares into half-square triangles.

■ One 5 1/2" square. Subcut the square into two half-square triangles. You will have one triangle left over.

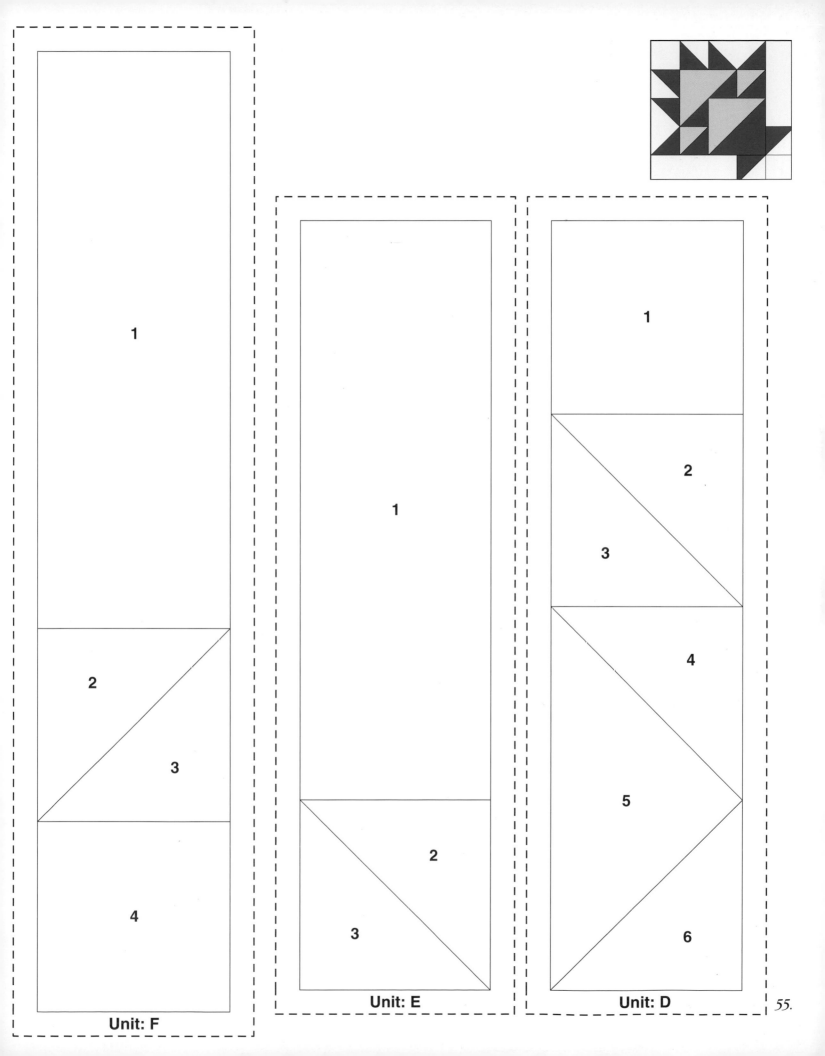

Unit: F

Unit: E

Unit: D

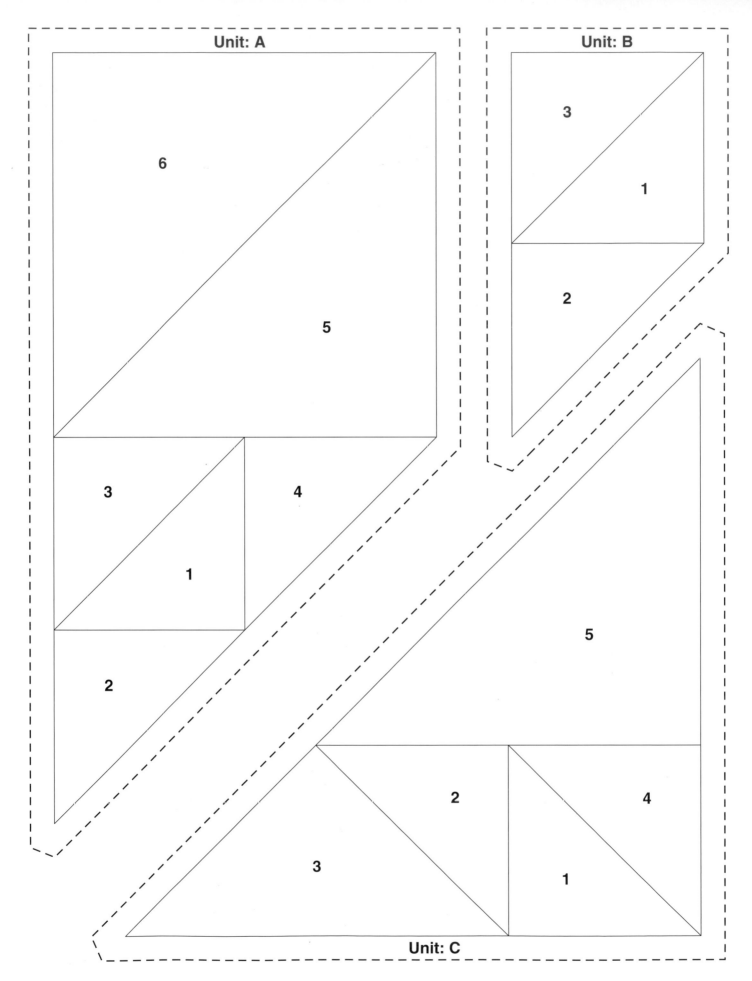

Unit: A

Unit: B

Unit: C

56. *May Basket in Floral Tones*

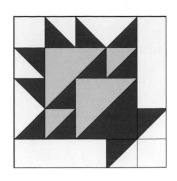

Position Chart

	Fabric	Position #	Size	
Unit A – Make 1			**10" Block**	
	Floral	1	3 1/2" x 3 1/2"	
	Green Vine	2,3,4	3 1/2" x 3 1/2"	
	Floral	5	5 1/2" x 5 1/2"	
	Green Vine	6	5 1/2" x 5 1/2"	
Unit B – Make 1				
	Floral	1	3 1/2" x 3 1/2"	
	Green Vine	2,3	3 1/2" x 3 1/2"	
Unit C – Make 1				
	Background	1	3 1/2" x 3 1/2"	
	Green Vine	2,4	3 1/2" x 3 1/2"	
	Background	3	4 3/4" x 4 3/4"	
	Floral	5	5 1/2" x 5 1/2"	
Unit D – Make 1				
	Background	1	3" x 3"	
	Green Vine	2,4,6	3 1/2" x 3 1/2"	
	Background	3	3 1/2" x 3 1/2"	
	Background	5	4 3/4" x 4 3/4"	
Unit E – Make 1				
	Background	1	3" x 6 3/4"	
	Green Vine	2	3 1/2" x 3 1/2"	
	Background	3	3 1/2" x 3 1/2"	
Unit F – Make 1				
	Background	1	3" x 6 3/4"	
	Green Vine	2	3 1/2" x 3 1/2"	
	Background	3	3 1/2" x 3 1/2"	
	Background	4	3" x 3"	

When putting the units together, see the instructions for the 4" block.

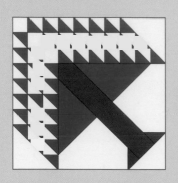

Pine Tree
September 1928
The Kansas City Star

Cutting Directions — Pine Tree 4" Block

From the light fabric, cut:

■ One 1 1/4" x 3 3/4" strip. Subcut the strip into three 1 1/4" squares.

■ One 1 1/2" x 27" strip. Subcut the strips into eighteen 1 1/2" squares. Cut the squares into half-square triangles.

■ One 2 1/2" x 5 1/2" strip. Subcut the strip into two 2 1/2" x 2 3/4" rectangles.

■ One 2 3/4" x 5 1/2" strip. Subcut the strip into two 2 3/4" squares. Cut the squares into half-square triangles.

From the green fabric, cut:

■ One 1 1/2" x 31 1/2" strip. Subcut the strip into twenty-one 1 1/2" squares. Cut the squares into half-square triangles.

■ One 2 3/4" square. Cut the square into half-square triangles.

From the brown fabric, cut:

■ One 1 1/2" square. Cut the square into half-square triangles.

■ One 1 1/2" x 4 1/2" strip.

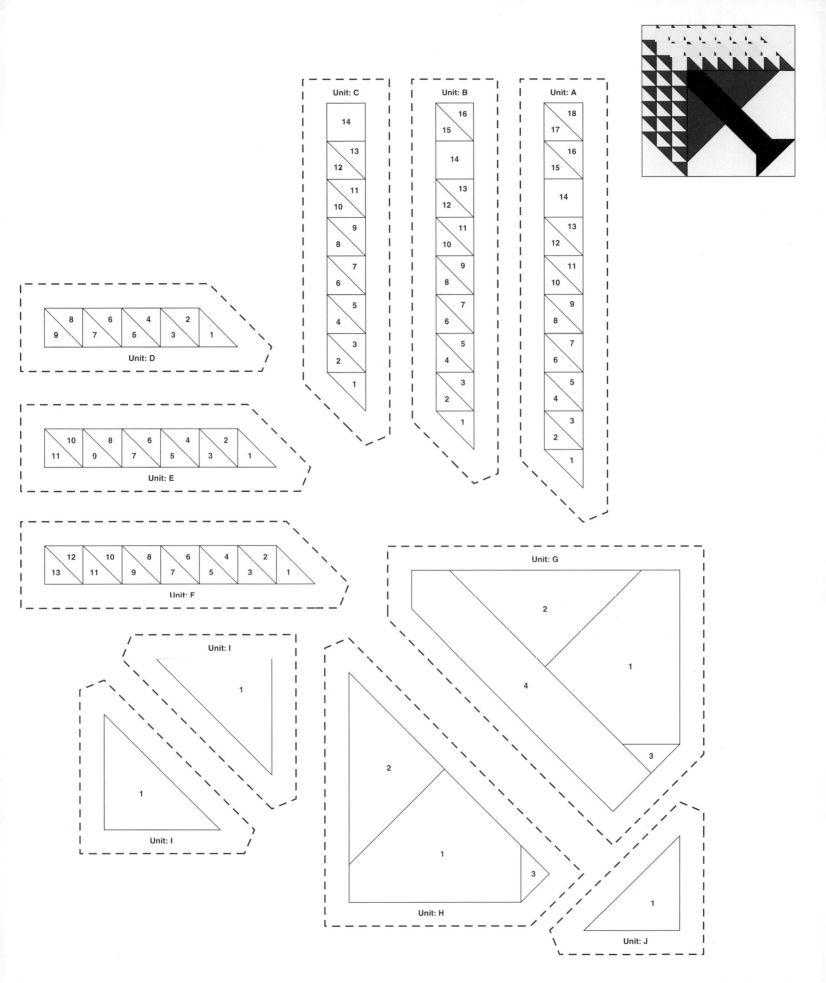

Unit: C

| 14 |
| 13 / 12 |
| 11 / 10 |
| 9 / 8 |
| 7 / 6 |
| 5 / 4 |
| 3 / 2 |
| 1 |

Unit: B

| 16 / 15 |
| 14 |
| 13 / 12 |
| 11 / 10 |
| 9 / 8 |
| 7 / 6 |
| 5 / 4 |
| 3 / 2 |
| 1 |

Unit: A

| 18 / 17 |
| 16 / 15 |
| 14 |
| 13 / 12 |
| 11 / 10 |
| 9 / 8 |
| 7 / 6 |
| 5 / 4 |
| 3 / 2 |
| 1 |

Unit: D

| 8 | 6 | 4 | 2 |
| 9 | 7 | 5 | 3 | 1 |

Unit: E

| 10 | 8 | 6 | 4 | 2 |
| 11 | 9 | 7 | 5 | 3 | 1 |

Unit: F

| 12 | 10 | 8 | 6 | 4 | 2 |
| 13 | 11 | 9 | 7 | 5 | 3 | 1 |

Unit: I

1

Unit: I

1
1

Unit: G

2
1
4
3

Unit: H

2
1
3

Unit: J

1

Pine Tree 59.

ASSEMBLING THE BLOCK:

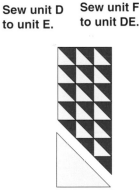

Sew unit A to unit B.

Sew unit C to unit AB.

Sew unit I to unit ABC.

Sew unit D to unit E.

Sew unit F to unit DE.

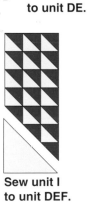

Sew unit I to unit DEF.

Fabric	Position #	Size	
4" Block			
Unit A,B,C – Make 1 of Each			
Green	ABC-1,3,5,7,9,11,13	1 1/2" x 1 1/2"	
Light	ABC-2,4,6,8,10,12	1 1/2" x 1 1/2"	
Light	ABC-14	1 1/4" x 1 1/4"	
Green	AB-15	1 1/2" x 1 1/2"	
Light	AB-16	1 1/2" x 1 1/2"	
Green	A-17	1 1/2" x 1 1/2"	
Light	A-18	1 1/2" x 1 1/2"	
Unit D,E,F – Make 1 of Each			
Green	DEF-1,3,5,7,9	1 1/2" x 1 1/2"	
Light	DEF-2,4,6,8	1 1/2" x 1 1/2"	
Light	EF-10	1 1/2" x 1 1/2"	
Green	EF-11	1 1/2" x 1 1/2"	
Light	F-12	1 1/2" x 1 1/2"	
Green	F-13	1 1/2" x 1 1/2"	
Unit G – Make 1			
Light	1	2 1/2" x 2 3/4"	
Green	2	2 3/4" x 2 3/4"	
Brown	3	1 1/2" x 1 1/2"	
Brown	4	1 1/4" x 4 1/2"	
Unit H– Make 1			
Light	1	2 1/2" x 2 3/4"	
Green	2	2 3/4" x 2 3/4"	
Brown	3	1 1/2" x 1 1/2"	
Unit I - Make 2			
Light	1	2 3/4" x 2 3/4"	
Unit J - Make 1			
Light	1	2 3/4" x 2 3/4"	

Sew unit G to unit H.

Sew unit J to unit GH.

Sew unit GHJ to unit DEFI.

Sew unit ABCI to unit DEFIGHJ.

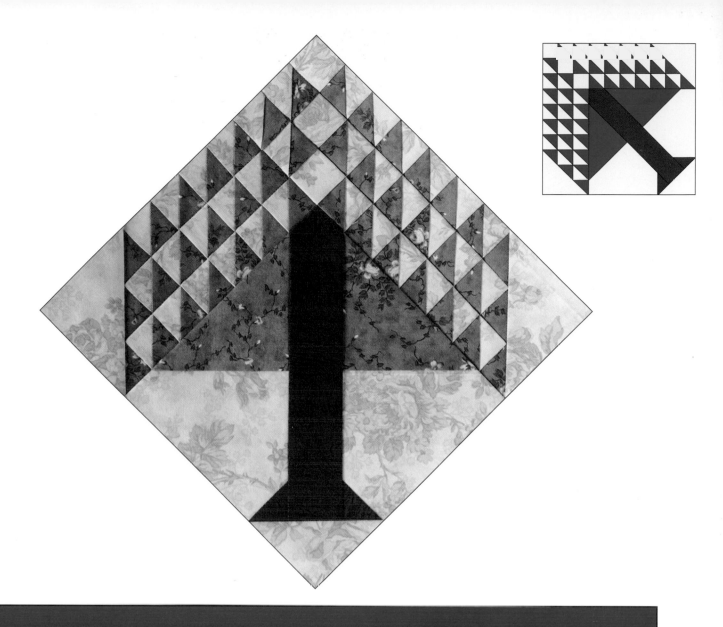

Cutting Directions — Pine Tree 10" Block

From the background fabric, cut:

■ One 2" x 6" strip. Subcut the strip into three 2" squares.

■ One 2 1/2" x 40" strip and one 2 1/2" x 5" strip. Subcut the strips into eighteen 2 1/2" squares. Cut the squares into half-square triangles.

■ One 4 3/4" x 20" strip. Subcut the strip into two 4 3/4" x 5 1/4" rectangles and two 4 3/4" squares. Cut the squares into half-square triangles. You will have one half-square triangle left over.

From the green fabric, cut:

■ One 2 1/2" x 40" strip and one 2 1/2" x 12 1/2" strip. Subcut the strips into twenty-one 2 1/2" squares. Cut the squares into half-square triangles.

■ Cut one 5 1/2" square. Cut the square into half-square triangles.

From the brown fabric, cut:

■ One 2 1/2" square. Cut the square into half-square triangles.

■ One 2 1/2" x 9 1/4" strip.

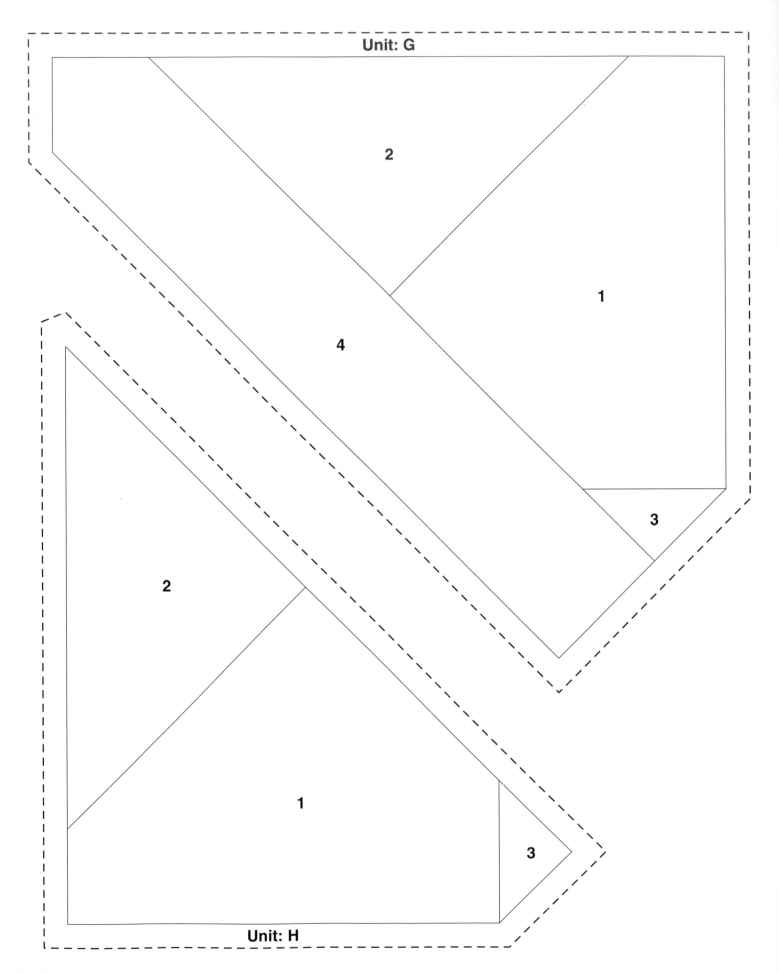

Unit: G

2

1

4

3

2

1

3

Unit: H

62. Pine Tree

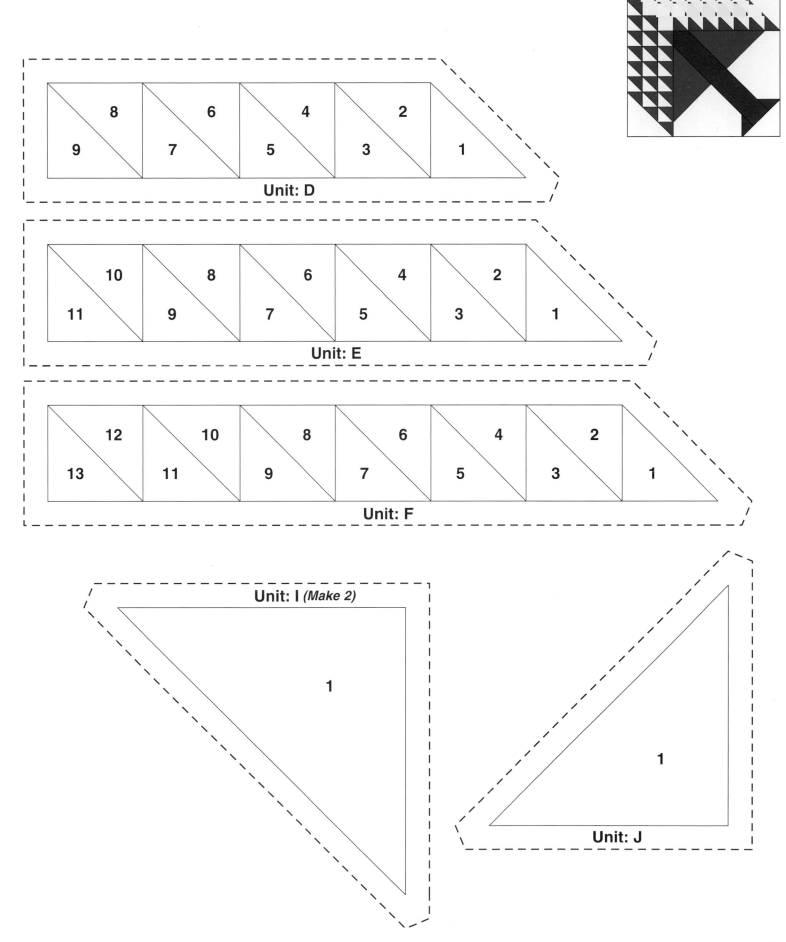

Unit: D

Unit: E

Unit: F

Unit: I *(Make 2)*

Unit: J

Pine Tree 63.

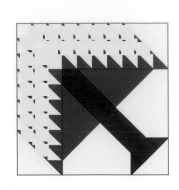

*P*ine *T*ree
September 1928
The Kansas City Star

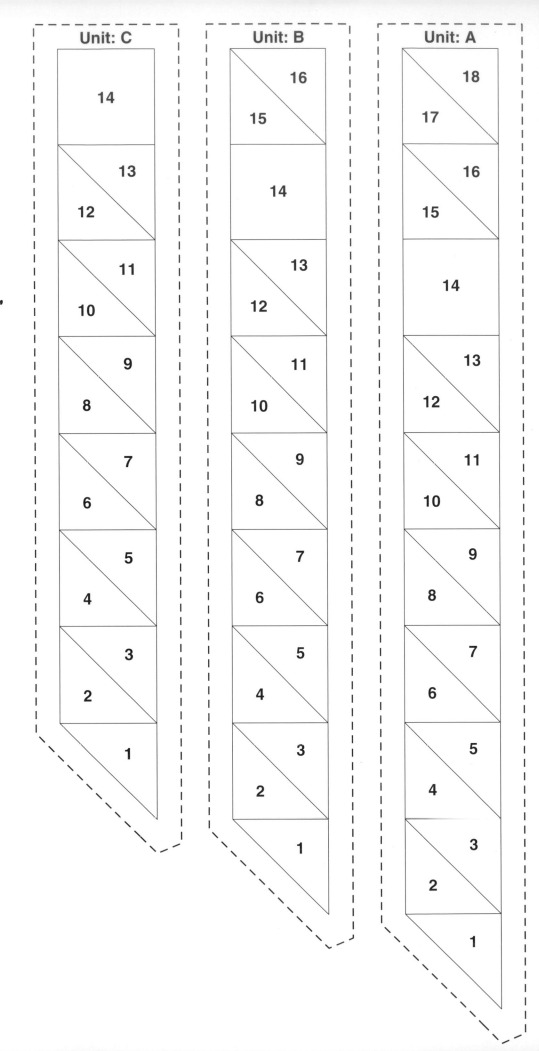

Unit: C

14
13
12
11
10
9
8
7
6
5
4
3
2
1

Unit: B

16
15
14
13
12
11
10
9
8
7
6
5
4
3
2
1

Unit: A

18
17
16
15
14
13
12
11
10
9
8
7
6
5
4
3
2
1

Position Chart — 10" Block

Fabric	Position #	Size	
Unit A,B,C - Make 1 of each			
Green	ABC-1,3,5,7,9,11,13	2 1/2" x 2 1/2"	◣
Background	ABC-2,4,6,8,10,12	2 1/2" x 2 1/2"	◣
Background	ABC-14	2" x 2"	
Green	AB-15	2 1/2" x 2 1/2"	◣
Background	AB-16	2 1/2" x 2 1/2"	◣
Green	A-17	2 1/2" x 2 1/2"	◣
Background	A-18	2 1/2" x 2 1/2"	◣
Unit D,E,F - Make 1 of each			
Green	DEF-1,3,5,7,9	2 1/2" x 2 1/2"	◣
Background	DEF-2,4,6,8	2 1/2" x 2 1/2"	◣
Background	EF-10	2 1/2" x 2 1/2"	◣
Green	EF-11	2 1/2" x 2 1/2"	◣
Background	F-12	2 1/2" x 2 1/2"	◣
Green	F-13	2 1/2" x 2 1/2"	◣
Unit G - Make 1			
Background	1	4 3/4" x 5 1/4"	
Green	2	5 1/2" x 5 1/2"	◣
Brown	3	2 1/2" x 2 1/2"	◣
Brown	4	2 1/2" x 9 1/4"	
Unit H - Make 1			
Background	1	4 3/4" x 5 1/4"	
Green	2	5 1/2" x 5 1/2'	◢
Brown	3	2 1/2" x 2 1/2"	◣
Unit I - Make 2			
Background	1	4 3/4" x 4 3/4"	◢
Unit J - Make 1			
Background	1	4 3/4" x 4 3/4"	◢

When you are ready to sew the units together, refer to the directions for the 4" block.

Pine Cone
October 1935
The Kansas City Star

Cutting Directions — Pine Cone 4" Block

From the light fabric, cut:

■ One 1" x 8" strip. Subcut the strip into eight 1" squares.

■ One 1 1/4" x 25" strip. Subcut the strip into twenty 1 1/4" squares. Cut the squares into half-square triangles.

■ One 2" x 16" strip. Subcut the strip into eight 2" squares. Cut four of the squares into half-square triangles.

■ One 1 3/4" x 7" strip. Subcut the strip into four 1 3/4" squares. Cut the squares into eight half-square triangles.

From the dark fabric, cut:

■ One 1 1/4" x 35" strip. Subcut the strip into twenty-eight 1 1/4" squares. Cut the squares into half-square triangles.

■ One 2" x 10" strip. Subcut the strip into five 2" squares. Cut four of the squares into half-square triangles.

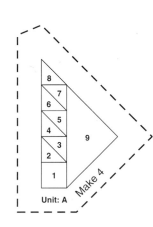

Pine Cone is the name of the pattern used in creating this lovely wall hanging pieced and quilted by Carolyn Cullinan McCormick.

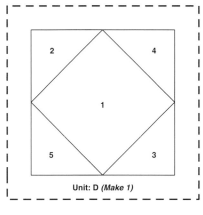

Unit: D *(Make 1)*

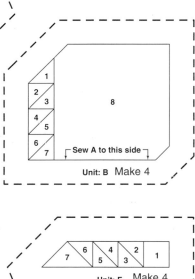

Unit: A Make 4

Unit: C Make 4

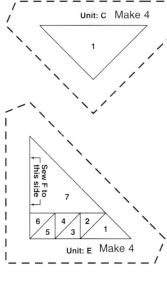

Sew F to this side

7

6 5 4 3 2 1

Unit: E Make 4

Unit: B Make 4

Sew A to this side

7 6 5 4 3 2 1

Unit: F Make 4

ASSEMBLING THE BLOCK:

Sew Unit A to Unit B (make 4 sets).

Sew Unit C to Unit AB (make 4 sets).

Sew Unit E to Unit F (make 4 sets).

Sew Unit EF on each side of Unit ABC as shown. (Make 2 sets)

Sew Unit ABC on two sides of Unit D as shown.

Sew the remaining Units together to complete the block.

*P*ine Cone
October 1935
The Kansas City Star

Fabric	Position #	Size
4" Block		
Unit A – Make 4		
Light	1	1" x 1"
Dark	2,4,6,8	1 1/4" x 1 1/4"
Light	3,5,7	1 1/4" x 1 1/4"
Dark	9	2" x 2"
Unit B – Make 4		
Dark	1,3,5,7	1 1/4" x 1 1/4"
Light	2,4,6	1 1/4" x 1 1/4"
Light	8	2" x 2"
Unit C – Make 4		
Dark	1	2" x 2"
Unit D – Make 1		
Dark	1	2" x 2"
Light	2,3,4,5	2" x 2"
Unit E – Make 4		
Light	1	1 3/4" x 1 3/4"
Dark	2,4,6	1 1/4" x 1 1/4"
Light	3,5	1 1/4" x 1 1/4"
Light	7	2" x 2"
Unit F – Make 4		
Light	1	1" x 1"
Dark	2,4,6	1 1/4" x 1 1/4"
Light	3,5	1 1/4" x 1 1/4"
Light	7	1 3/4" x 1 3/4"

Cutting Directions — Pine Cone 10" Block

From the background fabric, cut:

■ One 1 1/2" x 12" strip. Subcut the strip into eight 1 1/2" squares.

■ One 2" x 40" strip. Subcut the strip into twenty 2" squares. Cut the squares into half-square triangles.

■ One 4" x 16" strip. Subcut the strip into four 4" squares.

■ One 2 1/4" x 9" strip. Subcut the strip into four 2 1/4" squares. Cut the squares into half-square triangles.

■ One 3 1/2" x 14" strip. Subcut the strip into four 3 1/2" squares. Cut the squares into half-square triangles.

From the rose fabric, cut:

■ One 2" x 40" strip and one 2" x 16" strip. Subcut the strips into twenty-eight 2" squares. Cut the squares into half-square triangles.

■ One 3 1/2" x 17 1/2" strip. Subcut the strip into five 3 1/2" squares. Cut four of the squares into half-square triangles.

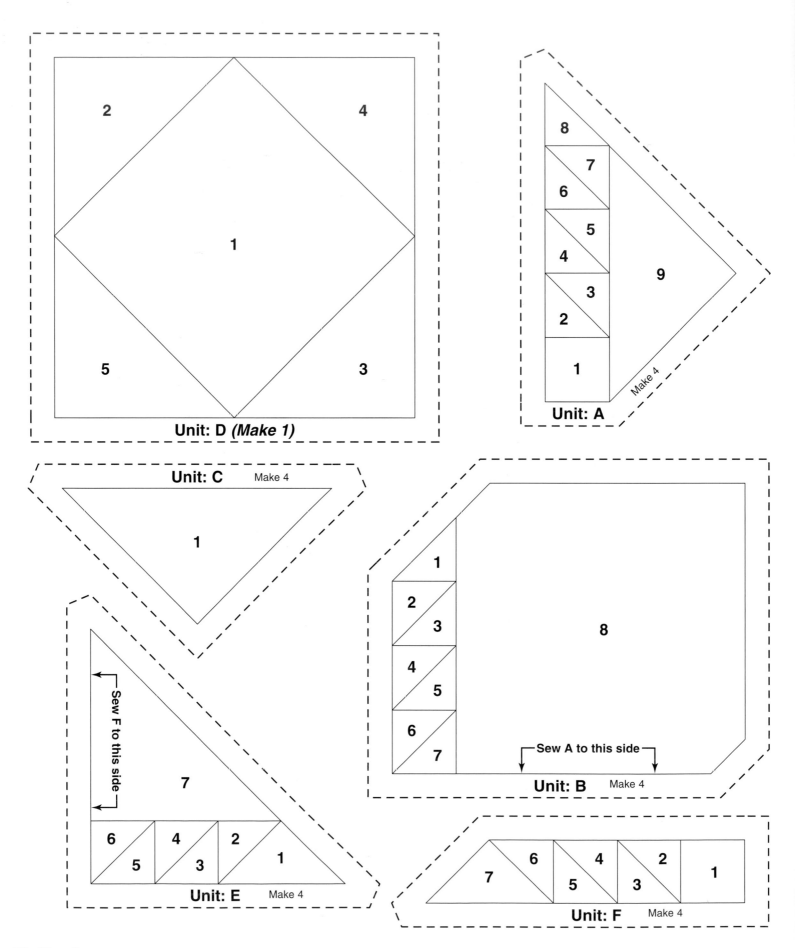

Unit: D (Make 1)

Unit: A   Make 4

Unit: C   Make 4

Sew F to this side

Unit: E   Make 4

Sew A to this side

Unit: B   Make 4

Unit: F   Make 4

70. Pine Cone

Position Chart — 10" Block

Fabric	Position #	Size	
Unit A – Make 4			
Background	1	1 1/2" x 1 1/2"	
Rose Solid	2,4,6,8	2" x 2"	◣
Background	3,5,7	2" x 2"	◪
Rose Solid	9	3 1/2" x 3 1/2"	◣
Unit B – Make 4			
Rose Solid	1,3,5,7	2" x 2"	◣
Background	2,4,6	2" x 2"	◪
Background	8	4" x 4"	
Unit C – Make 4			
Rose Solid	1	3 1/2" x 3 1/2"	◣
Unit D – Make 1			
Rose Solid	1	3 1/2" x 3 1/2"	
Background	2,3,4,5	3 1/2 x 3 1/2"	◣
Unit E – Make 4			
Background	1	2 1/4" x 2 1/4"	◣
Rose Solid	2,4,6	2" x 2"	◣
Background	3,5	2" x 2"	◪
Background	7	3 1/2" x 3 1/2	◣
Unit F – Make 4			
Background	1	1 1/2" x 1 1/2"	
Rose Solid	2,4,6	2" x 2"	◣
Background	3,5	2" x 2"	◪
Background	7	2 1/4" x 2 1/4"	◣

When you are ready to put the units together, refer to the directions for the 4" block.

Christmas Tree

June 1934
The Kansas City Star

Cutting Directions — Christmas Tree 4" Block

From the light fabric, cut:

■ One 1 1/2" x 4 1/2" strip. Subcut the strip into three 1 1/2" squares.

■ One 1 3/4" x 10 1/2" strip. Subcut the strip into six 1 3/4" squares. Cut the squares into half-square triangles.

■ One 2 3/4" square and one 3 1/4" square. Cut both squares into half-square triangles.

From the dark fabric, cut:

■ One 1 3/4" x 15 3/4" strip. Subcut the strip into nine 1 3/4" squares. Cut the squares into half-square triangles.

■ One 1" x 4" rectangle.

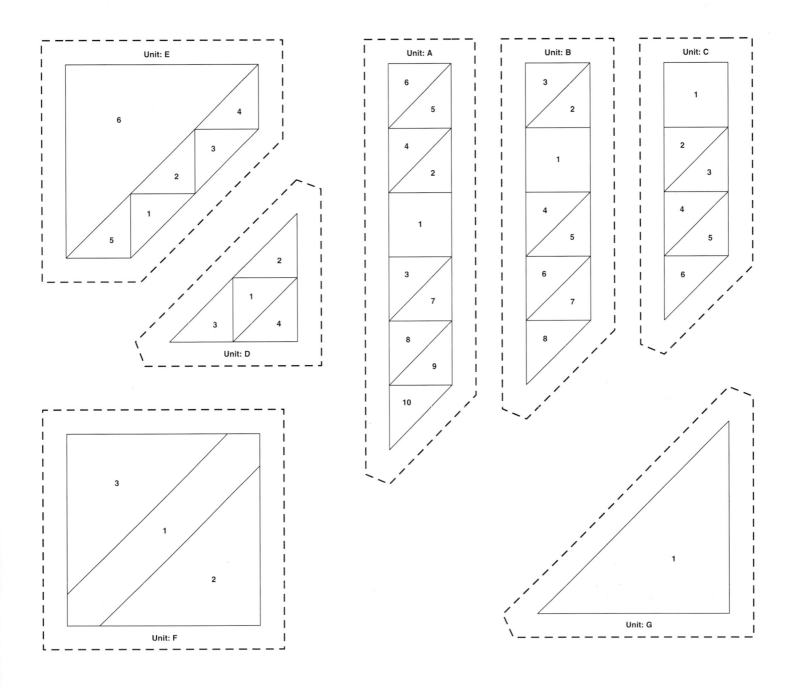

Unit: E

Unit: D

Unit: A

Unit: B

Unit: C

Unit: F

Unit: G

Christmas Tree

June 1934
The Kansas City Star

Position Chart

	Fabric	Position #	Size
4" Block			
Unit A – Make 1			
	Light	1	1 1/2" x 1 1/2"
	Dark	2,3,5,8,10	1 3/4" x 1 3/4"
	Light	4,6,7,9	1 3/4" x 1 3/4"
Unit B – Make 1			
	Light	1	1 1/2" x 1 1/2"
	Dark	2,4,6,8	1 3/4" x 1 3/4"
	Light	3,5,7	1 3/4" x 1 3/4"
Unit C – Make 1			
	Light	1	1 1/2" x 1 1/2"
	Dark	2,4,6	1 3/4" x 1 3/4"
	Light	3,5	1 3/4" x 1 3/4"
Unit D – Make 1			
	Light	1	1 3/4" x 1 3/4"
	Dark	2,3,4	1 3/4" x 1 3/4"
Unit E – Make 1			
	Light	1,3	1 3/4" x 1 3/4"
	Dark	2,4,5	1 3/4" x 1 3/4"
	Light	6	3 1/4" x 3 1/4"
Unit F – Make 1			
	Dark	1	1" x 4"
	Light	2,3	2 3/4" x 2 3/4"
Unit G – Make 1			
	Light	1	3 1/4" x 3 1/4"

ASSEMBLING THE BLOCK:

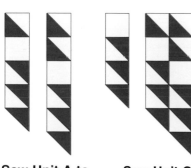

Sew Unit A to Unit B.

Sew Unit C to Unit AB.

Sew Unit G to Unit ABC.

Sew Unit D to Unit E.

Sew Unit F to Unit DE.

Sew Unit ABCG to Unit DEF.

Cutting Directions — Christmas Tree 10" Block

From the background fabric, cut:

■ One 2 1/2" x 7 1/2" strip. Subcut the strip into three 2 1/2" squares.

■ One 3" x 18" strip. Subcut the strip into six 3" squares. Cut the squares into half-square triangles.

■ One 5 3/4" square and one 6 3/4" square. Cut both squares into half-square triangles.

From the green fabric, cut:

■ One 3" x 27" strip. Subcut the strip into nine 3" squares. Cut the squares into half-square triangles.

■ One 2" x 8" rectangle.

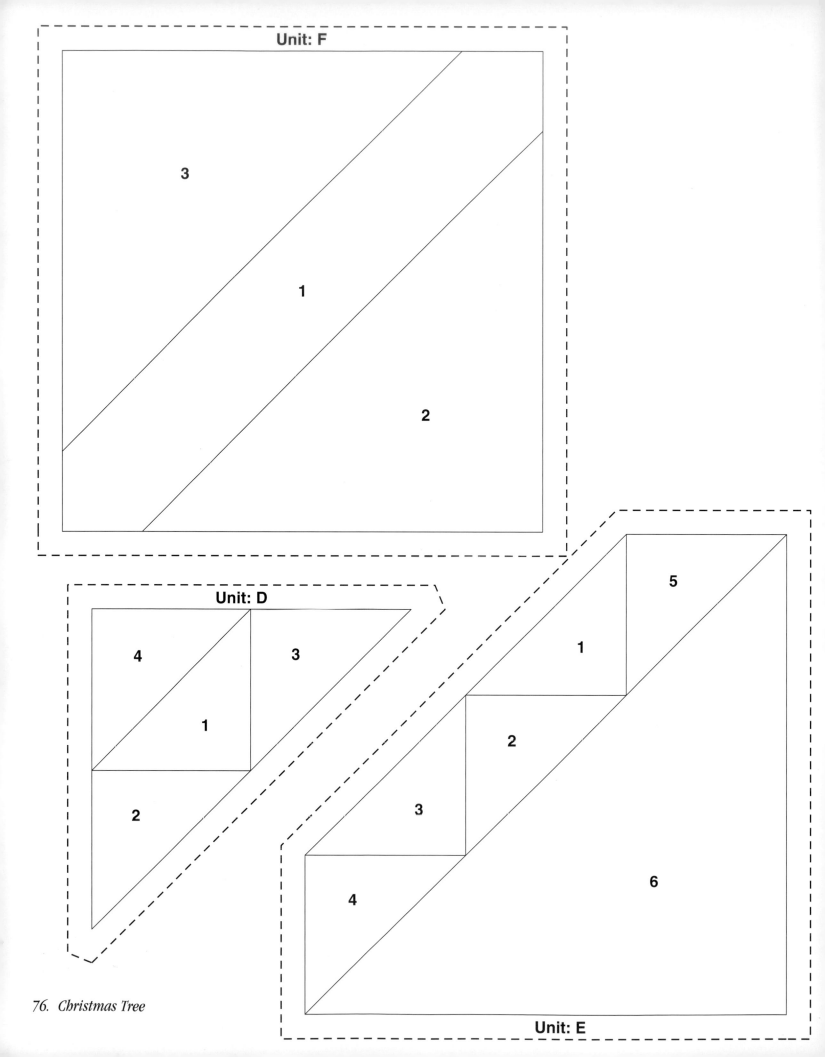

Unit: F

3

1

2

Unit: D

4

3

1

2

5

1

2

3

4

6

76. *Christmas Tree*

Unit: E

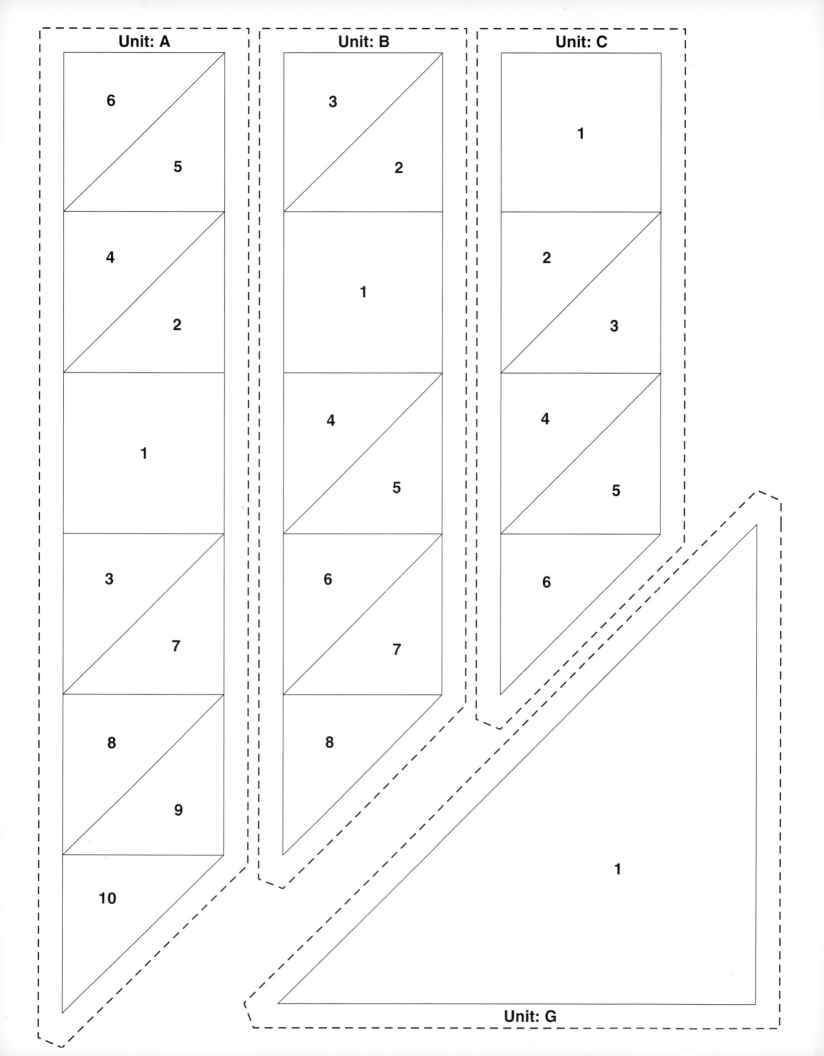

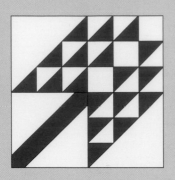

Christmas Tree

June 1934
The Kansas City Star

	Fabric	Position #	Size	
10" Block				
Unit A – Make 1				
	Background	1	2 1/2" x 2 1/2"	
	Green Solid	2,3,5,8,10	3" x 3"	
	Background	4,6,7,9	3" x 3"	
Unit B – Make 1				
	Background	1	2 1/2" x 2 1/2"	
	Green Solid	2,4,6,8	3" x 3"	
	Background	3,5,7	3" x 3"	
Unit C – Make 1				
	Background	1	2 1/2" x 2 1/2"	
	Green Solid	2,4,6	3" x 3"	
	Background	3,5	3" x 3"	
Unit D – Make 1				
	Background	1	3" x 3"	
	Green Solid	2,3,4	3" x 3"	
Unit E – Make 1				
	Background	1,3	3" x 3"	
	Green Solid	2,4,5	3" x 3"	
	Background	6	6 3/4" x 6 3/4"	
Unit F – Make 1				
	Green Solid	1	2" x 8"	
	Background	2,3	5 3/4" x 5 3/4"	
Unit G – Make 1				
	Background	1	6 3/4" x 6 3/4"	

When you are ready to sew the units together, refer to the instructions for the 4" block.

Sage Bud
November 1930
The Kansas City Star

Cutting Directions — Sage Bud 4" Block

From the light fabric, cut:

■ One 1" x 4" strip. Subcut the strip into four 1" squares.

■ One 1 3/4" x 7" strip. Subcut the strip into four 1 3/4" squares. Cut the squares into half-square triangles.

■ One 2 1/4" x 9" strip. Cut the strip into four 2 1/4" squares.

From the medium fabric, cut:

■ One 1 3/4" x 7" strip. Subcut the strip into four 1 3/4" squares. Cut

the squares into half-square triangles.

From the dark rose fabric, cut:

■ One 3/4" x 12" strip. Subcut the strip into 3/4" x 3" rectangles.

From the dark green fabric, cut:

■ One 2" x 4" strip. Subcut the strip into two 2" squares. Cut the squares into half-square triangles.

■ One 2 1/4" square.

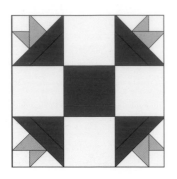

*S*age *B*ud
November 1930
The Kansas City Star

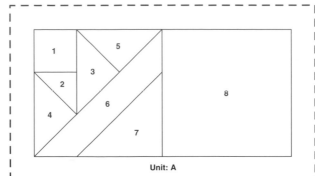

Unit: A

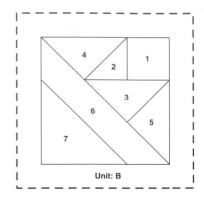

Unit: B

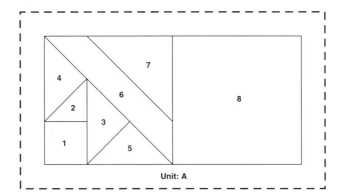

Unit: C

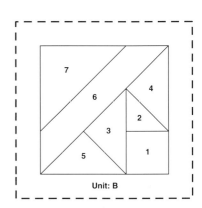

Unit: A

Unit: B

ASSEMBLING THE BLOCK:

Sew Unit A to Unit B. You will need to make two of each.

Sew each to the top and bottom of Unit C to complete the block.

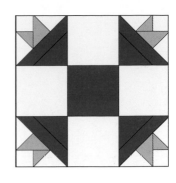

Position Chart	4" Block	
Fabric	**Position #**	**Size**
Unit A – Make 2		
Light	1	1" X 1"
Medium	2,3	1 3/4" x 1 3/4"
Light	4,5	1 3/4" x 1 3/4"
Dark Rose	6	3/4" x 3"
Dark Green	7	2" x 2"
Light	8	2 1/4" x 2 1/4"
Unit B – Make 2		
Light	1	1" x 1"
Medium	2,3	1 3/4" x 1 3/4"
Light	4,5	1 3/4" x 1 3/4"
Dark Rose	6	3/4" x 3"
Dark Green	7	2" x 2"
Unit C – Make 1		
Light	1,3	2 1/4" x 2 1/4"
Dark Green	2	2 1/4" x 2 1/4"

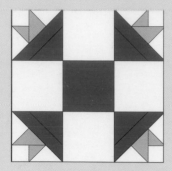

Sage Bud
November 1930
The Kansas City Star

Cutting Directions — Sage Bud 10" Block

From the background fabric, cut:

■ One 2" x 8" strip. Subcut the strip into four 2" squares.

■ One 3" x 12" strip. Subcut the strip into four 3" squares. Cut the squares into half-square triangles.

■ One 4 1/4" x 17" strip. Subcut the strip into four 4 1/4" squares.

From the solid rose fabric, cut:

■ One 2 3/4" x 11" strip. Subcut the strip into four 2 3/4" squares. Cut the squares into half-square triangles.

From the dark rose fabric, cut:

■ One 1 1/2" x 24" strip. Subcut the strip into four 1 1/2" x 6" rectangles.

From the green fabric, cut:

■ One 3 1/2" x 7" strip. Subcut the strip into two 3 1/2" squares. Cut the squares into half-square triangles.

■ One 4 1/2" square.

Unit: C *(Make 1)*

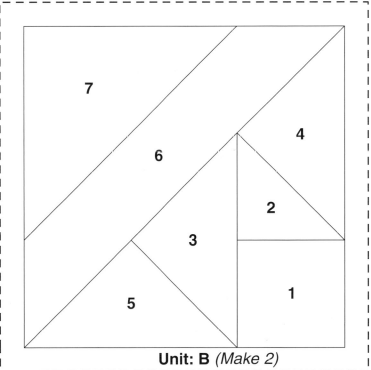

Unit: B *(Make 2)*

Sage Bud 83.

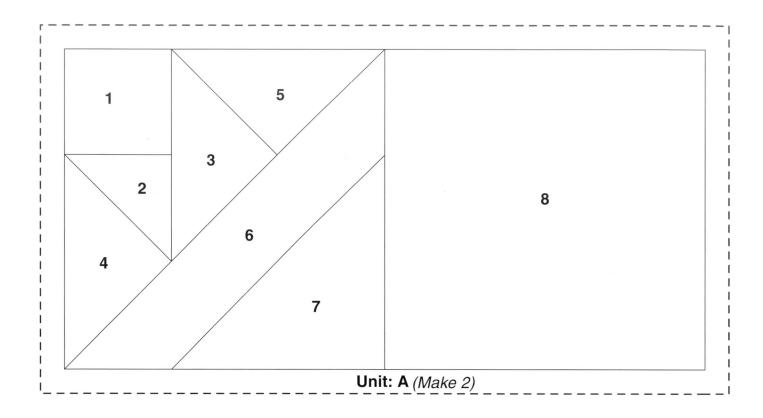

Unit: A *(Make 2)*

See the instructions for the 4" block when you are ready to sew the units together.

		10" Block
Fabric	**Position #**	**Size**
Unit A – Make 2		
Background	1	2" x 2"
Rose Solid	2,3	2 3/4"x 2 3/4"
Background	4,5	3" x 3"
Rose	6	1 1/2" x 6"
Green Vine	7	3 1/2" x 3 1/2"
Background	8	4 1/4" x 4 1/4"
Unit B – Make 2		
Background	1	2" x 2"
Rose Solid	2,3	2 3/4" x 2 3/4"
Background	4,5	3" x 3"
Rose	6	1 1/2" x 6"
Green Vine	7	3 1/2" x 3 1/2"
Unit C – Make 1		
Background	1,3	4 1/4" x 4 1/4"
Green Vine	2	4 1/4" x 4 1/4"

Garden Walk
June 1940
The Kansas City Star

Cutting Directions — Garden Walk 4" Block

From the light fabric, cut:

■ One 2" x 8" strip. Subcut the strip into four 2" squares.

■ One 1 1/4" x 13" strip.**

From the dark fabric, cut:

■ One 1 1/4" x 20" strip. Subcut the strip into eight 1 1/4" x 2 1/2" rectangles.

■ One 1 1/4" x 13" strip.**

** Sew the light 1 1/4" x 13" strip to the dark 1 1/4" x 13" strip using a 1/8" seam allowance. Press towards the dark fabric. Cut the strip into 1 1/4" pieces. You will need 10 pieces.

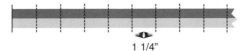

1 1/4"

These pieces are indicated on the patterns by double pointed arrows.

Garden Walk

June 1940
The Kansas City Star

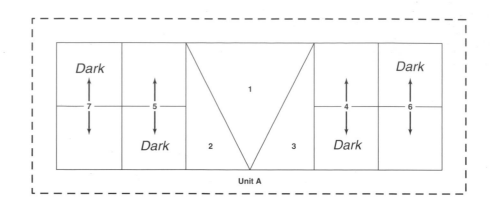

Unit A

Dark — 7
Dark — 5
1
2   3
Dark — 4
Dark — 6

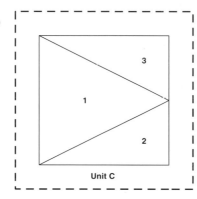

Unit C

1
3
2

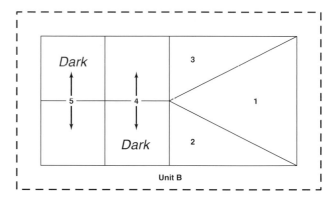

Unit B

Dark — 5
Dark — 4
3
1
2

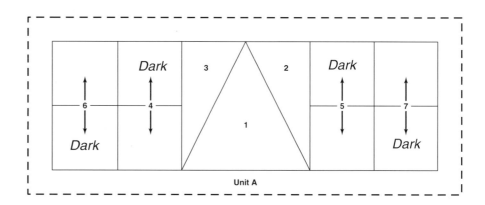

Unit A

Dark — 6
Dark
Dark — 4
3   2
1
Dark — 5
Dark
Dark — 7
Dark

ASSEMBLING THE BLOCK:

Sew Unit B to Unit C. This makes
the center of the block.

Sew the Unit As to the Unit BC as
shown to complete the block.

Patrice Heath, Parker, Colorado, made this table runner using the Garden Walk pattern.

Fabric	Position #	Size
4" Block		
Unit A – Make 2		
Light	1	2" x 2"
Dark	2,3	1 1/4" x 2 1/2"
Dark/Light	4,5,6,7	**
Unit B – Make 1		
Light	1	2" x 2"
Dark	2,3	1 1/4" x 2 1/2"
Dark/Light	4,5	**
Unit C – Make 1		
Light	1	2" x 2"
Dark	2,3	1 1/4" x 2 1/2"

** See cutting instructions.

Garden Walk
June 1940
The Kansas City Star

Cutting Directions — Garden Walk 10" Block

From the background fabric, cut:

■ One 4 1/4" x 17" strip. Subcut the strip into four 4 1/4" squares.

■ One 2 1/2" x 26" strip.**

From the rose fabric, cut:

■ One 2 1/2" x 40" strip. Subcut the strip into eight 2 1/2" x 5" rectangles.

■ One 2 1/2" x 26" strip.**

** Sew the light 2 1/2" x 26" strip to the dark 2 1/2" x 26" strip using a 1/4" seam allowance. Press towards the dark fabric. Cut the strip into 2 1/2" pieces. You will need 10 pieces.

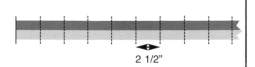

2 1/2"

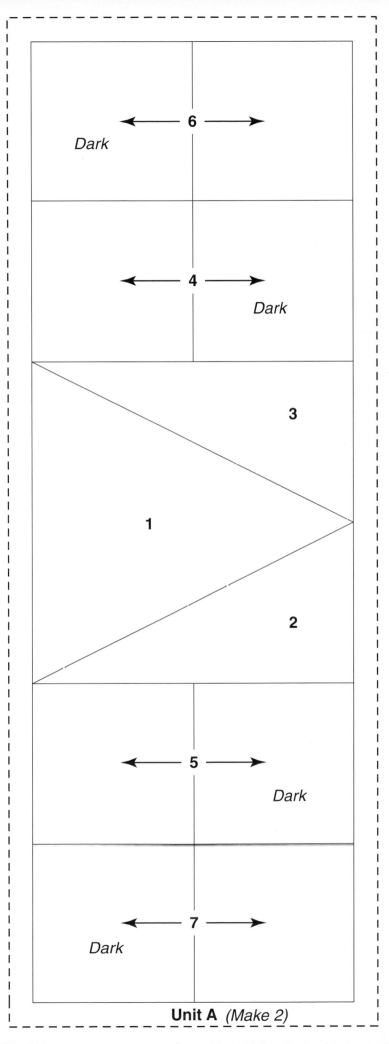

Dark

← 6 →

← 4 →

Dark

3

1

2

Unit A *(Make 2)*

← 5 →

Dark

← 7 →

Dark

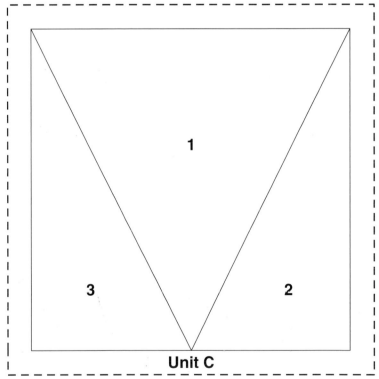

1

3

2

Unit C

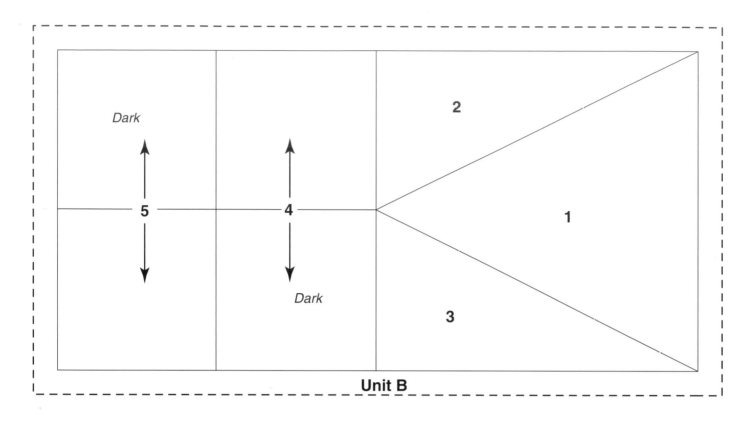

Unit B

		10" Block	
Fabric	**Position #**	**Size**	
Unit A – Make 2			
Background	1	4 1/4" x 4 1/4"	
Rose	2,3	2 1/2" x 5"	
Rose/			
Background	4,5,6,7	**	
Unit B – Make 1			
Background	1	4 1/4" x 4 1/4"	
Rose	2,3	2 1/2" x 5"	
Rose/			
Background	4,5	**	
Unit C – Make 1			
Background	1	4 1/4" x 4 1/4"	
Rose	2,3	2 1/2" x 5"	

** *See cutting instructions.*

When you are ready to sew the units together, refer to the directions for the 4" block.

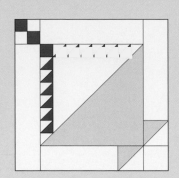

Hanging Basket

August 1937
The Kansas City Star

Cutting Directions — Hanging Basket 4" Block

From the light fabric, cut:

■ One 1 1/2" x 25 3/4" strip. Subcut the strip into eight 1 1/2" squares, two 1 1/2" x 3 1/2" rectangles, one 1 1/2" x 2 3/4" rectangle and one 1 1/2" x 4" rectangle. Cut the seven squares into half-square triangles.

■ One 3 1/4" square. Cut the square into half-square triangles. You will have one half-square triangle left over.

■ One 2" square. Cut the square into half-square triangles.

■ One 1" x 2 1/2" strip ***

From the dark fabric, cut:

■ One 1" x 3 1/2" strip. Subcut the strip into one 1" square and one 1" x 2 1/2" strip.***

■ One 1 1/2" x 9" strip. Subcut the strip into six 1 1/2" squares. Cut the squares into half-square triangles.

From the floral fabric, cut:

■ One 2" square. Cut the square into half-square triangles.

■ One 4" square. Cut the square into half-square triangles. You will have one half-square triangle left over.

*** Sew the light 1" x 2 1/2" strip to the dark 1" x 2 1/2" strip. Press towards the dark fabric and cut into two 1" pieces.

1"

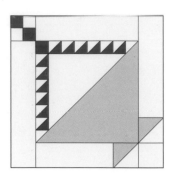

*H*anging *B*asket
August 1937
The Kansas City Star

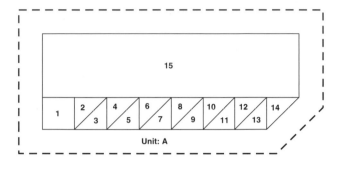

Unit: A

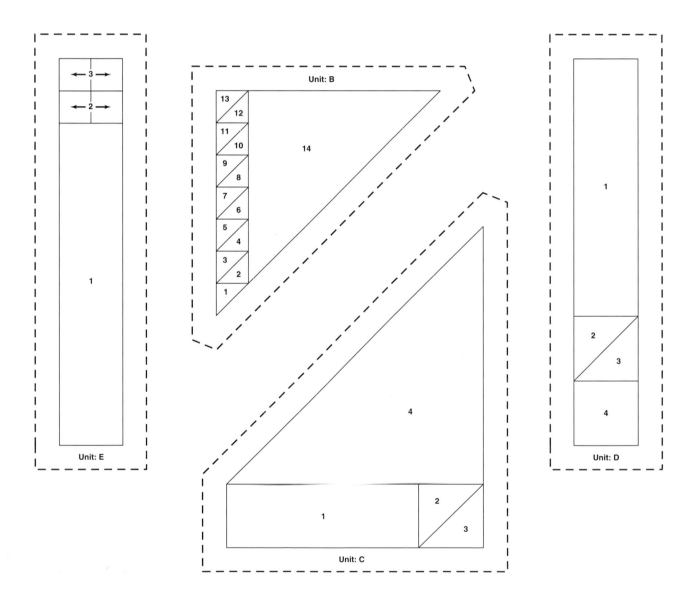

92. *Hanging Basket*

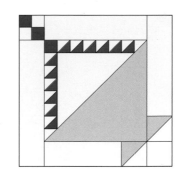

4" Block

Fabric	Position #	Size	
Unit A – Make 1			
Dark	1	1" x 1"	
Light	2,4,6,8,10,12,14	1 1/2" x 1 1/2"	◣
Dark	3,5,7,9,11,13	1 1/2" x 1 1/2"	◣
Light	15	1 1/2" x 3 1/2"	
Unit B – Make 1			
Light	1,3,5,7,9,11,13	1 1/2" x 1 1/2"	◣
Dark	2,4,6,8,10,12	1 1/2" x 1 1/2"	◣
Light	14	3 1/4" x 3 1/4"	◣
Unit C – Make 1			
Light	1	1 1/2" x 2 3/4"	
Floral	2	2" x 2"	◣
Light	3	2" x 2"	◣
Floral	4	4" x 4"	◣
Unit D – Make 1			
Light	1	1 1/2" x 3 1/2"	
Floral	2	2" x 2"	◣
Light	3	2" x 2"	◣
Light	4	1 1/2" x 1 1/2"	
Unit E – Make 1			
Light	1	1 1/2" x 4"	
Light/Dark	2,3	*	

* See cutting directions.

ASSEMBLING THE BLOCK:

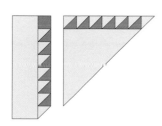

Sew Unit A to Unit B.

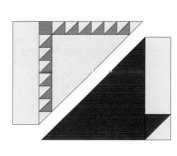

Sew Unit C to Unit AB.

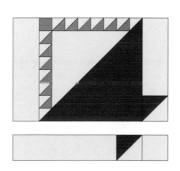

Add Unit D as shown.

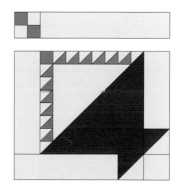

Now sew on Unit E to complete the block.

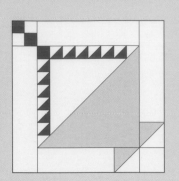

Hanging Basket
August 1937
The Kansas City Star

Cutting Directions — Hanging Basket 10" Block

From the background fabric, cut:

■ One 2 1/4" x 15 3/4" strip. Subcut the strip into seven 2 1/4" squares. Cut the squares into half-square triangles.

■ One 2 1/2" x 32 3/4" strip. Subcut the strip into two 2 1/2" x 7 1/2" rectangles, one 2 1/2" x 6" rectangle, one 2 1/2" x 9 1/4" rectangle and one 2 1/2" square.

■ One 6 3/4" square. Cut the square into half-square triangles. You will have one triangle left over.

■ One 3 1/4" square. Cut the square into half-square triangles.

■ One 1 1/2" x 3" strip*

From the green solid fabric, cut:

■ One 1 3/4" square.

■ One 2 1/4" x 13 1/2" strip. Subcut the strip into six 2 1/4" squares. Cut the squares into half-square triangles.

■ One 1 1/2" x 3" strip.*

From the floral fabric, cut:

■ One 3 1/4" square. Cut the square into half-square triangles

■ One 8 1/2" square. Cut the square into half-square triangles. You will have one triangle left over.

*Sew the background 1 1/2" x 3" strip to the green 1 1/2" x 3" strip. Press towards the dark fabric and cut into two 1 1/2" pieces.

1 1/2"

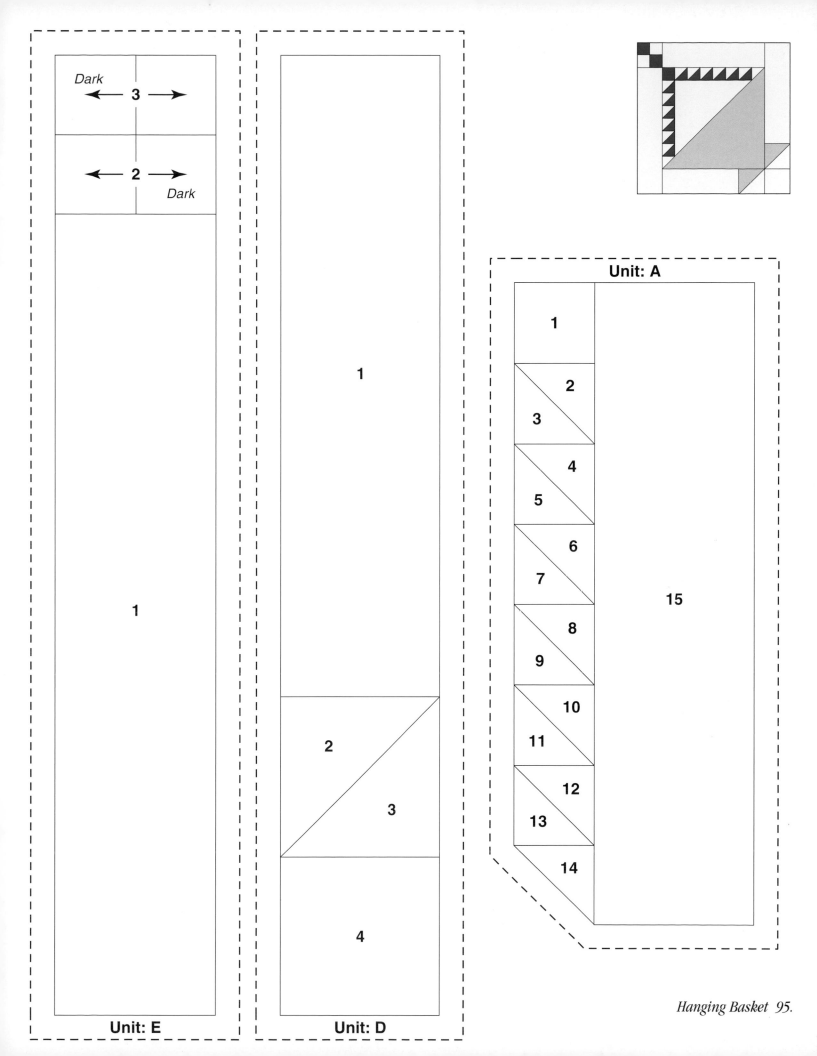

Unit: E

Dark
← 3 →

← 2 →
Dark

1

Unit: D

1

2

3

4

Unit: A

1

2

3

4

5

6

7

8

9

10

11

12

13

14

15

Hanging Basket 95.

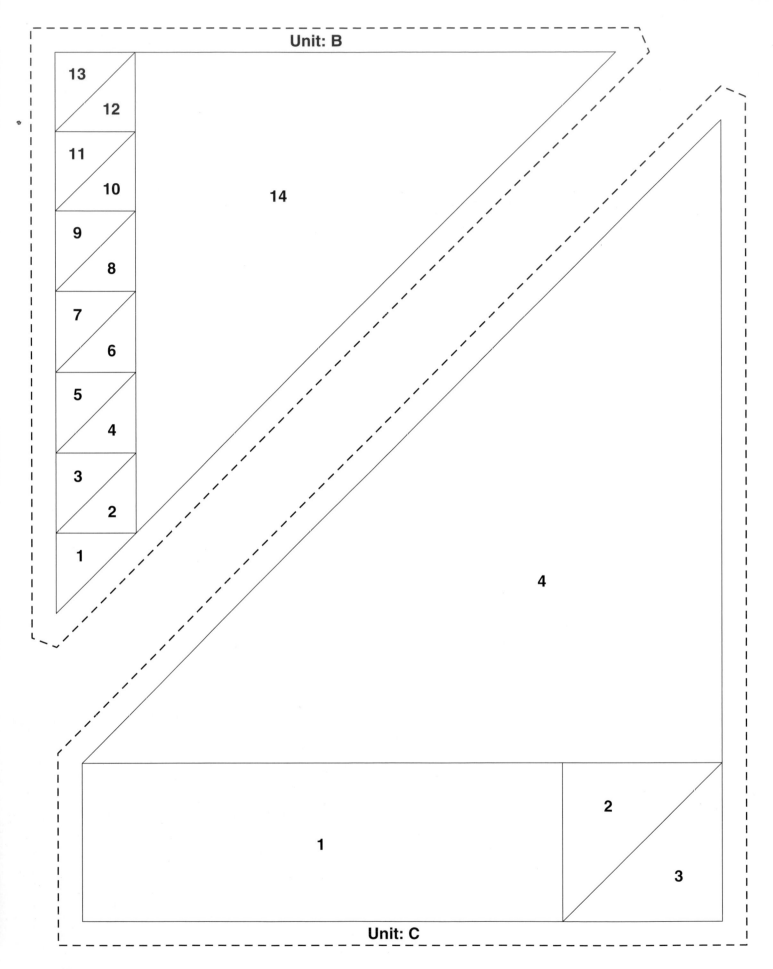

96. *Hanging Basket*

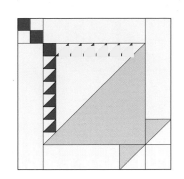

Position Chart — 10" Block

Fabric	Position #	Size	
Unit A – Make 1			
Green Solid	1	1 3/4" x 1 3/4"	
Background	2,4,6,8,10,12,14	2 1/4" x 2 1/4"	◣
Green Solid	3,5,7,9,11,13	2 1/4" x 2 1/4"	◣
Background	15	2 1/2" x 7 1/2"	
Unit B – Make 1			
Background	1,3,5,7,9,11,13	2 1/4" x 2 1/4"	◣
Green Solid	2,4,6,8,10,12	2 1/4" x 2 1/4"	◣
Background	14	6 3/4" x 6 3/4"	◣
Unit C – Make 1			
Background	1	2 1/2" x 6"	
Floral	2	3 1/4" x 3 1/4"	◣
Background	3	3 1/4" x 3 1/4"	◣
Floral	4	8 1/2" x 8 1/2"	◣
Unit D – Make 1			
Background	1	2 1/2" x 7 1/2"	
Floral	2	3 1/4" x 3 1/4"	◣
Background	3	3 1/4" x 3 1/4"	◣
Background	4	2 1/2" x 2 1/2"	
Unit E – Make 1			
Background	1	2 1/2" x 9 1/4"	
Green/ Background	2,3	*	

* See cutting directions.

To sew the units together, follow the directions for the
4" block.

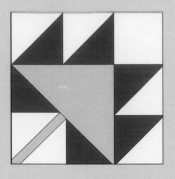

Apple Leaf
September 1935
The Kansas City Star

The miniature Apple Leaf quilt was pieced and quilted by Carolyn Cullinan McCormick.

Cutting Directions — Apple Leaf 4" Block

From the light fabric, cut:

■ One 2 1/2" x 7 1/2" strip. Subcut the strip into three 2 1/2" squares. Cut the squares into six half-square triangles.

■ One 2 1/4" square.

From the floral fabric, cut:

■ One 3/4" x 3" strip.

■ One 4" square. Cut the square into two half-square triangles. You will have one triangle left over.

From the dark green fabric, cut:

■ One 2 1/2" x 7 1/2" strip. Subcut the strip into three 2 1/2" squares. Cut the squares into six half-square triangles.

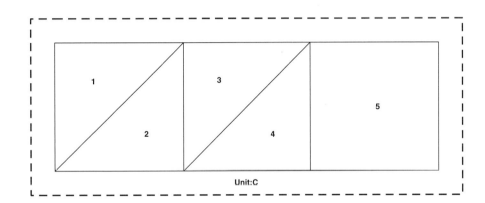

Unit:C

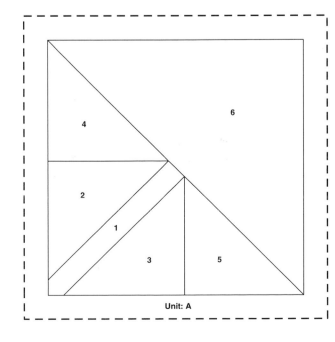

Unit: A

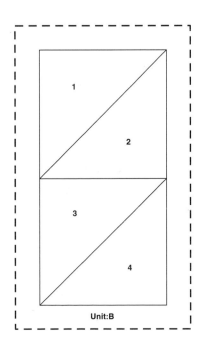

Unit:B

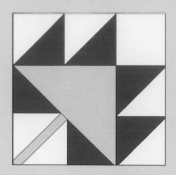

Apple Leaf

September 1935
The Kansas City Star

Position Chart

Position Chart		4" Block
Fabric	**Position #**	**Size**
Unit A – Make 1		
Floral	1	3/4" x 3"
Light	2,3	2 1/2" x 2 1/2" 
Dark Green	4,5	2 1/2" x 2 1/2"
Floral	6	4" x 4"
Unit B – Make 1		
Dark Green	1,3	2 1/2" x 2 1/2"
Light	2,4	2 1/2" x 2 1/2"
Unit C – Make 1		
Light	1,3	2 1/2" x 2 1/2"
Dark Green	2,4	2 1/2" x 2 1/2"
Light	5	2 1/4" x 2 1/4"

ASSEMBLING THE BLOCK:

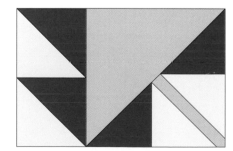

Sew Unit A to Unit B.

Add Unit C to complete the block.

Cutting Directions — Apple Leaf 10" Block

From the background fabric, cut:

■ One 5" x 15" strip. Subcut the strip into three 5" squares. Cut the squares into six half-square triangles.

■ One 4 1/4" square.

From the green leaves fabric, cut:

■ One 1 1/4" x 5 1/2" strip.

■ One 8 3/4" x 8 3/4" square. Cut the square into two half-square triangles. You will have one half-square triangle left over.

From the green vine fabric, cut:

■ One 5" x 15" strip. Subcut the strip into three 5" squares. Cut the squares into six half-square triangles.

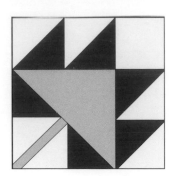

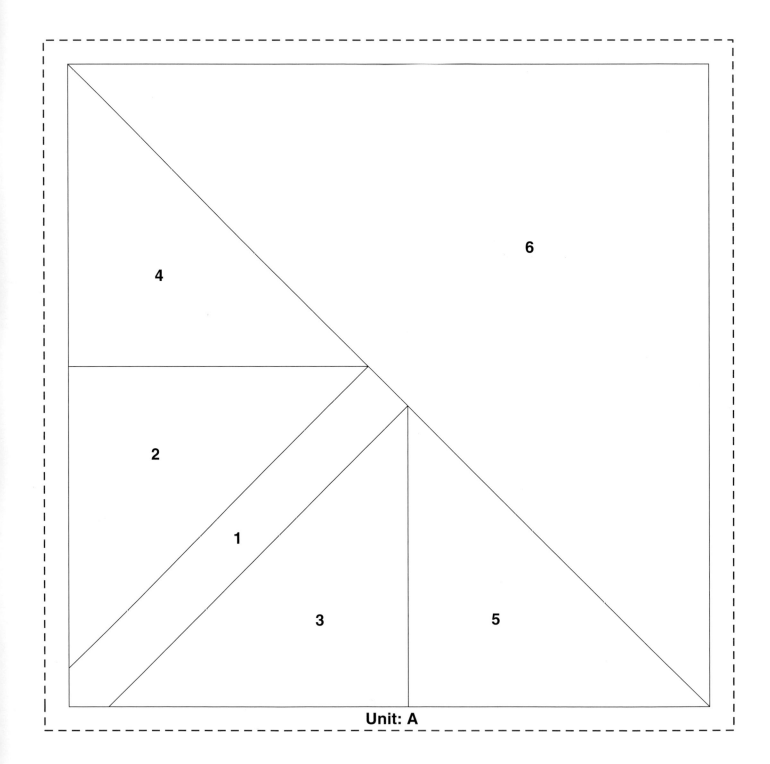

Unit: A

102. *Apple Leaf*

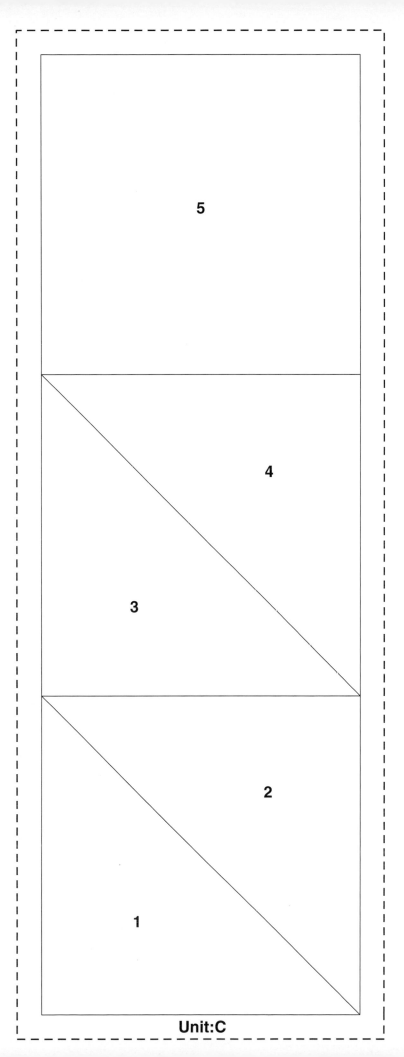

5

4

3

2

1

Unit:C

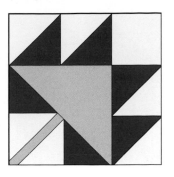

Apple Leaf 103.

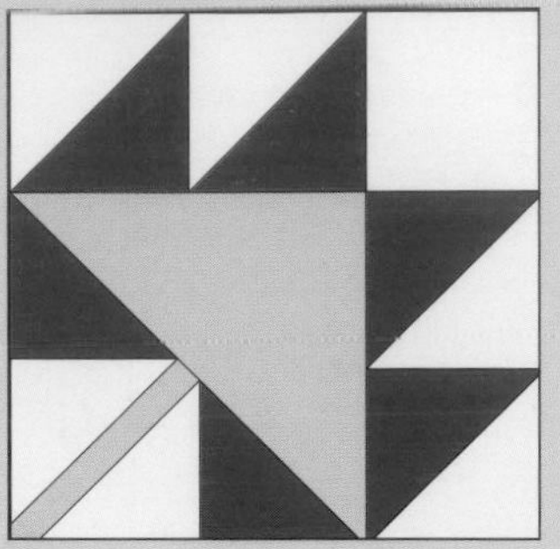

*A*pple *L*eaf

September 1935
The Kansas City Star

Position Chart — 10" Block

Fabric	Position #	Size
Unit A – Make 1		
Green Leaves	1	1 1/4" x 5 1/2"
Background	2,3	5" x 5"
Green Vine	4,5	5" x 5"
Green Leaves	6	8 3/4" x 8 3/4"
Unit B – Make 1		
Green Vine	1,3	5" x 5"
Background	2,4	5" x 5"
Unit C – Make 1		
Background	1,3	5" x 5"
Green Vine	2,4	5" x 5"
Background	5	4 1/4" x 4 1/4"

To sew the units together, follow the directions for the 4" block.

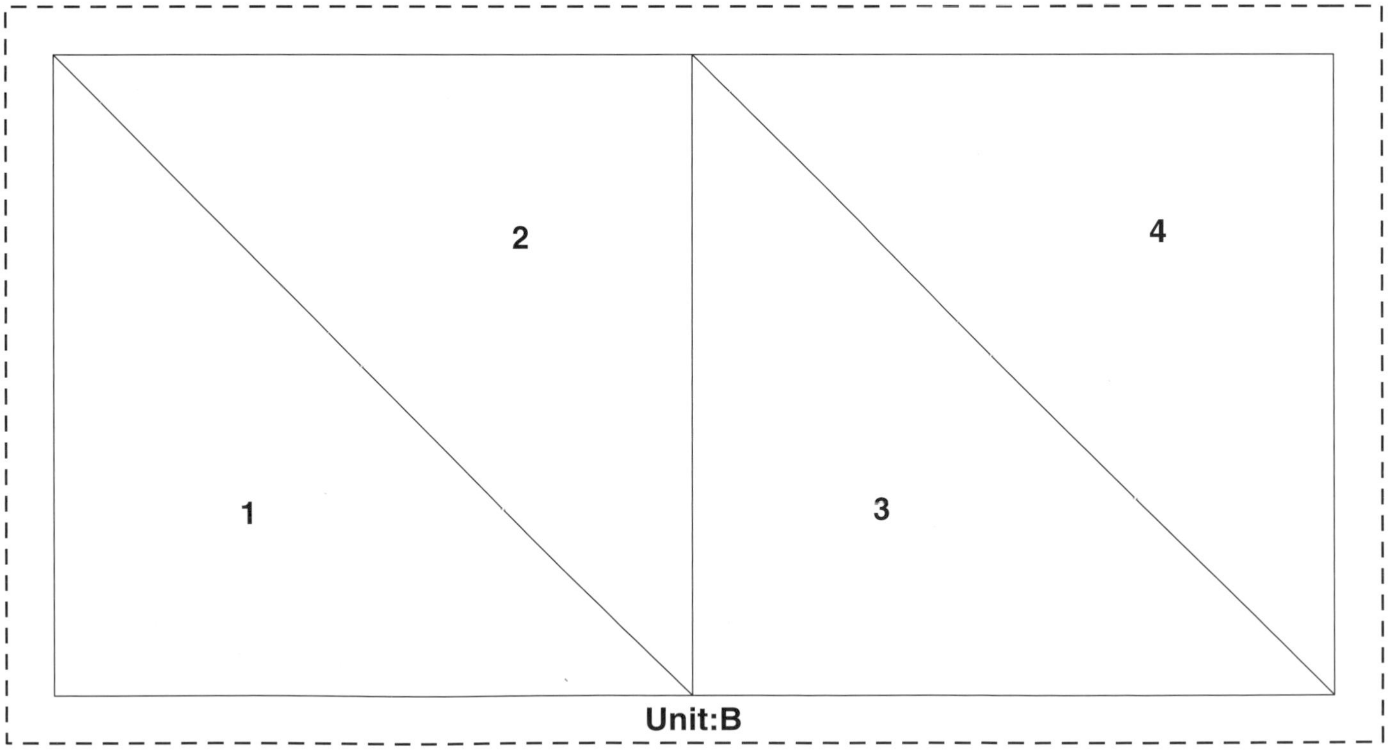

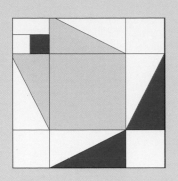

Magnolia Bud
March 1932
The Kansas City Star

From the light fabric, cut:

■ One 1" square.

■ One strip 1" x 1 3/4."

■ One strip 1 3/4" x 5 1/4." Subcut the strip into three 1 3/4" squares.

■ One strip 1 1/2" x 12." Subcut the strip into four 1 1/2" x 3" rectangles.

From the floral fabric, cut:

■ One 2 3/4" square.

■ One 1 1/2" x 6" strip. Subcut the strip into two 1 1/2" x 3" rectangles.

From the green fabric, cut:

■ One 1" square.

■ One 1 1/2" x 6" strip. Subcut the strip into two 1 1/2" x 3" rectangles.

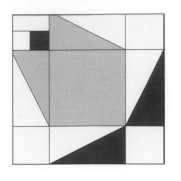

Magnolia Bud

March 1932
The Kansas City Star

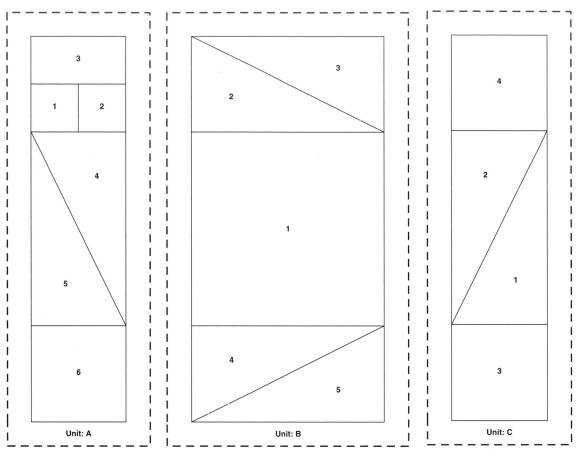

Unit: A

Unit: B

Unit: C

ASSEMBLING THE BLOCK:

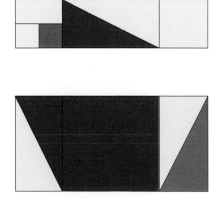

Sew Unit A to Unit B.

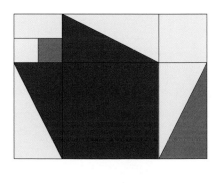

Add Unit C to complete the block.

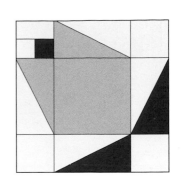

	Fabric	Position #	Size
			4" Block
	Fabric	Position #	Size
Unit A – Make 1			
	Light	1	1" x 1"
	Dark Green	2	1" x 1"
	Light	3	1" x 1 3/4"
	Floral	4	1 1/2" x 3"
	Light	5	1 1/2" x 3"
	Light	6	1 3/4" x 1 3/4"
Unit B – Make 1			
	Floral	1	2 3/4" x 2 3/4"
	Floral	2	1 1/2" x 3"
	Light	3,4	1 1/2" x 3"
	Dark Green	5	1 1/2" x 3"
Unit C – Make 1			
	Dark Green	1	1 1/2" x 3"
	Light	2	1 1/2" x 3"
	Light	3,4	1 3/4" x 1 3/4"

Position Chart

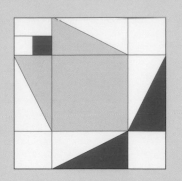

Magnolia Bud
March 1932
The Kansas City Star

Cutting Directions — Magnolia Bud 10" Block

From the background fabric, cut:

■ One 2" x 2" square.

■ One 2" x 3 1/2" strip.

■ One 3 1/2" x 37 1/2" strip. Subcut the strip into three 3 1/2" squares and four 6 3/4" x 3 1/2" rectangles.

From the floral fabric, cut:

■ One 6" square.

■ One 3 1/2" x 12" strip. Cut the strip into two 3 1/2" x 6" rectangles.

From the green fabric, cut:

■ One 2" square.

■ One 3 1/2" x 13 1/2" strip. Subcut the strip into two 3 1/2" x 6 3/4" rectangles.

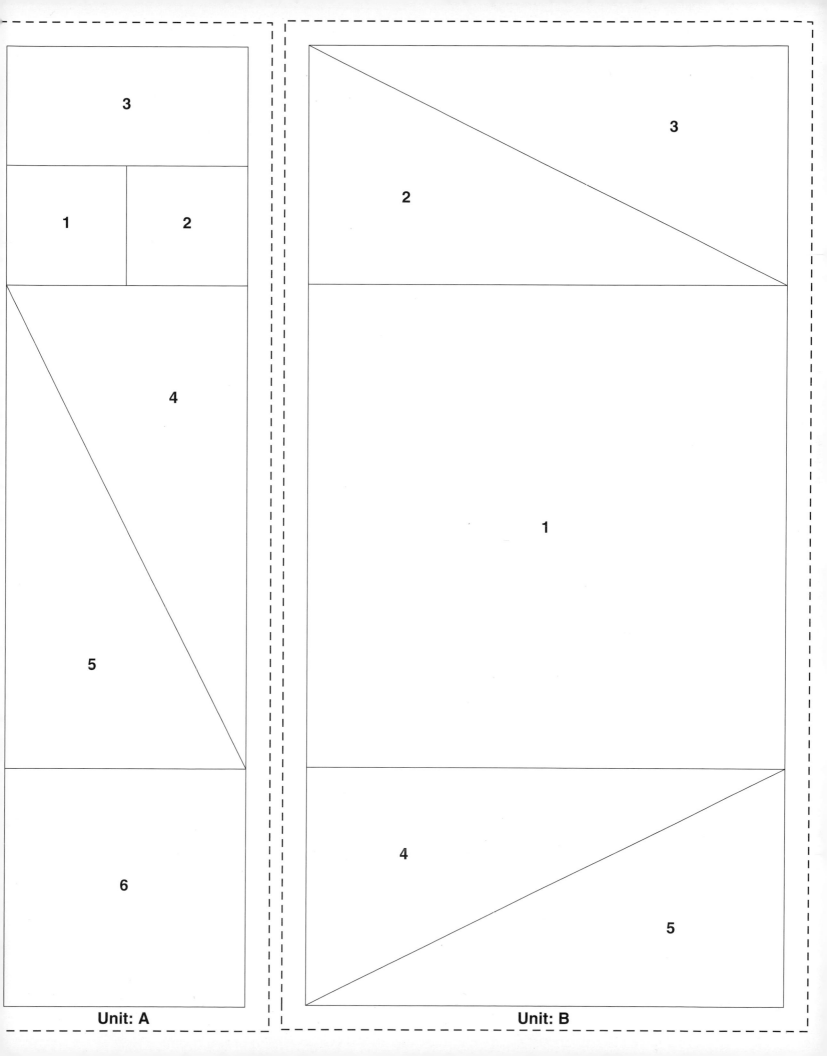

Unit: A

Unit: B

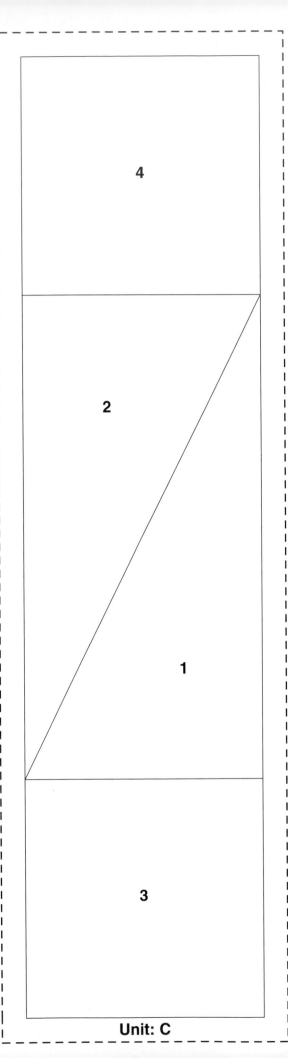

Unit: C

Position Chart — **10" Block**

Fabric	Position #	Size
Unit A – Make 1		
Background	1	2" x 2"
Green Solid	2	2" x 2"
Background	3	2" x 3 1/2"
Floral	4	3 1/2" x 6"
Background	5	3 1/2" x 6 3/4"
Background	6	3 1/2" x 3 1/2"
Unit B – Make 1		
Floral	1	6" X 6"
Floral	2	6" X 3 1/2"
Background	3,4	3 1/2" x 6 3/4"
Green Solid	5	3 1/2" x 6 3/4"
Unit C – Make 1		
Green Solid	1	3 1/2" x 6 3/4"
Background	2	3 1/2" x 6 3/4"
Background	3,4	3 1/2" x 3 1/2"

To sew the units together, follow the directions for the 4" block.

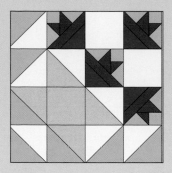

Basket of Lilies
April 1931
The Kansas City Star

From the light fabric, cut:

■ One 2" x 4" strip. Cut the strip into two 2" squares.

■ One 2 1/4" x 9" strip. Subcut the strip into four 2 1/4" squares. Cut the squares into half-square triangles. You will have one triangle left over.

From the medium fabric, cut:

■ One 1" x 4" strip. Subcut the strip into four 1" squares.

■ One 1 1/2" x 6" strip. Subcut the strip into four 1 1/2" squares. Cut the squares into half-square triangles.

■ One 2 1/4" x 9" strip. Subcut

the strip into four 2 1/4" squares. Cut the squares into half-square triangles. You will have one triangle left over.

From the dark green fabric, cut:

■ One 1 3/4" x 3 1/2" strip. Subcut the strip into two 1 3/4" squares. Cut the squares into half-square triangles.

From the dark rose fabric, cut:

■ One 1 1/2" x 6" strip. Subcut the strip into four 1 1/2" squares. Cut the squares into half-square triangles.

■ One 3/4" x 10" strip. Subcut the strip into four 3/4" x 2 1/2" rectangles.

From the floral fabric, cut:

■ One 2 1/4" x 4 1/2" strip. Subcut the strip into two 2 1/4" squares. Cut the squares into half-square triangles.

■ One 2" square.

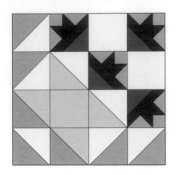

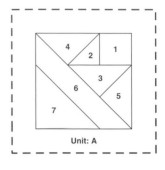

Unit: A

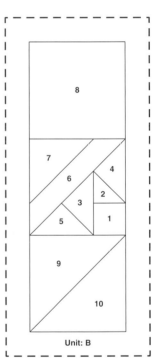

Unit: B

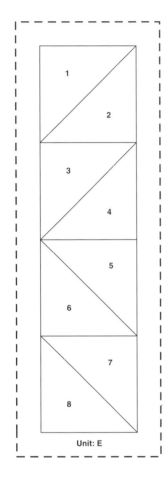

Unit: E

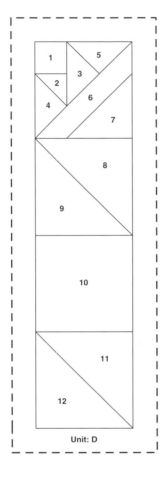

Unit: D

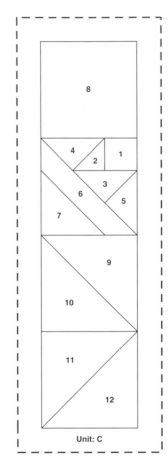

Unit: C

ASSEMBLING THE BLOCK:

Sew Unit B to Unit A.

Add Unit C as shown.

Next sew Unit D in place.

Add Unit E to complete the block.

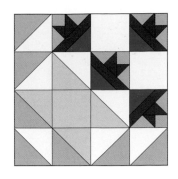

Position Chart

		4" Block	
Fabric	**Position #**	**Size**	
Unit A – Make 1			
Medium	1	1" x 1"	
Dark	2,3	1 1/2" x 1 1/2"	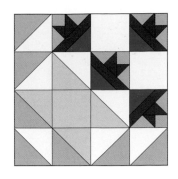
Medium	4,5	1 1/2" x 1 1/2"	
Dark	6	3/4" x 2 1/2"	
Dark Green	7	1 3/4" x 1 3/4"	
Unit B – Make 1			
Medium	1	1" x 1"	
Dark	2,3	1 1/2" x 1 1/2"	
Medium	4,5	1 1/2" x 1 1/2"	
Dark	6	3/4" x 2 1/2"	
Dark Green	7	1 3/4" x 1 3/4"	
Light	8	2" x 2"	
Light	9	2 1/4" x 2 1/4"	
Medium	10	2 1/4" x 2 1/4"	
Unit C – Make 1			
Medium	1	1" x 1"	
Dark	2,3	1 1/2" x 1 1/2"	
Medium	4,5	1 1/2" x 1 1/2"	
Dark	6	3/4" x 2 1/2"	
Dark Green	7	1 3/4" x 1 3/4"	
Light	8	2" x 2"	
Light	9,11	2 1/4" x 2 1/4"	
Floral	10	2 1/4" x 2 1/4"	
Medium	12	2 1/4" x 2 1/4"	
Unit D - Make 1			
Medium	1	1" x 1"	
Dark	2,3	1 1/2" x 1 1/2"	
Medium	4,5	1 1/2" x 1 1/2"	
Dark	6	3/4" x 2 1/2"	
Dark Green	7	1 3/4" x 1 3/4"	
Light	8	2 1/4" x 2 1/4"	
Floral	9,11	2 1/4" x 2 1/4"	
Floral	10	2" x 2"	
Medium	12	2 1/4" x 2 1/4"	
Unit E - Make 1			
Medium	1,3,6,8	2 1/4" x 2 1/4"	
Light	2,4,7	2 1/4" x 2 1/4"	
Floral	5	2 1/4" x 2 1/4"	

Basket of Lilies 113.

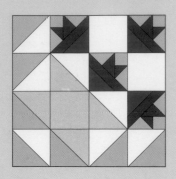

*B*asket of *L*ilies
April 1931
The Kansas City Star

Cutting Directions — Basket of Lilies 10" Block

From the background fabric, cut:

■ One 3 1/4" x 6 1/2" strip. Cut the strip into two 3 1/4" squares.

■ One 4" x 16" strip. Subcut the strip into four 4" squares. Cut the squares into half-square triangles. You will have one triangle left over.

From the green solid fabric, cut:

■ One 1 3/4" x 7" strip. Subcut the strip into four 1 3/4" squares.

■ One 2 1/2" x 10" strip. Subcut the strip into four 2 1/2" squares.

Cut the squares into half-square triangles.

■ One 4" x 16" strip. Subcut the strip into four 4" squares. Cut the squares into half-square triangles. You will have one triangle left over.

From the green vine fabric, cut:

■ One 3 1/4" x 6 1/2" strip. Subcut the strip into two 3 1/4" squares. Cut the squares into half-square triangles.

From the rose solid fabric, cut:

■ One 2 1/2" x 10" strip. Subcut

the strip into four 2 1/2" squares. Cut the squares into half-square triangles.

From the dark rose fabric, cut:

■ One 1 1/4" x 18" strip. Subcut the strip into four 1 1/4" x 4 1/2" rectangles.

From the floral fabric, cut:

■ One 4" x 8" strip. Subcut the strip into two 4" squares. Cut the squares into half-square triangles.

■ One 3 1/4" square.

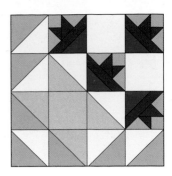

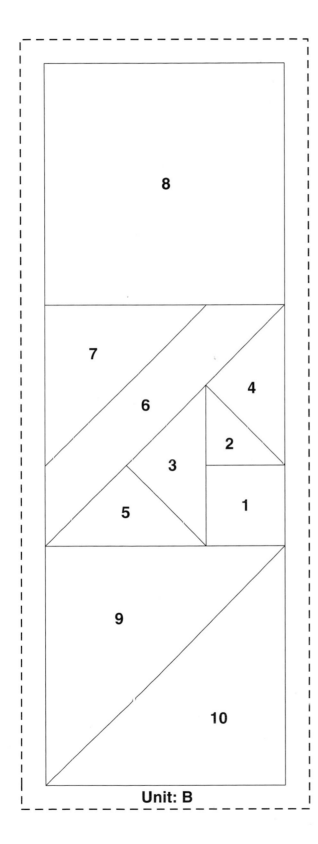

Unit: B

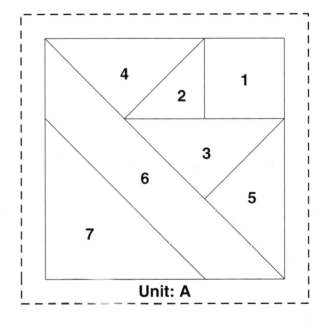

Unit: A

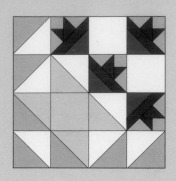

Basket of **L**ilies
April 1931
The Kansas City Star

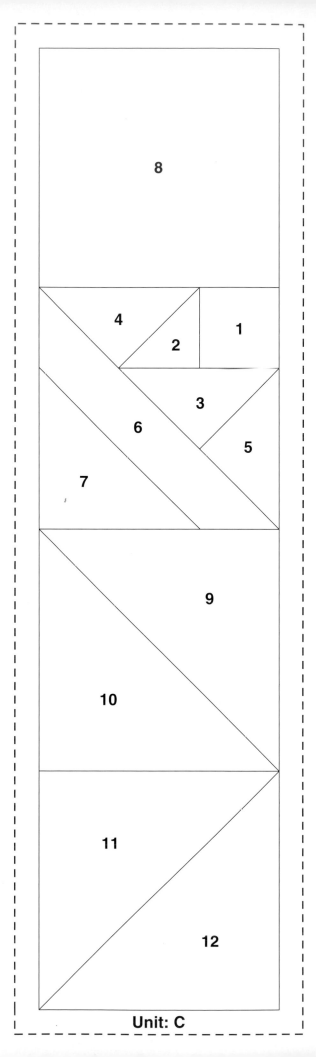

Unit: C

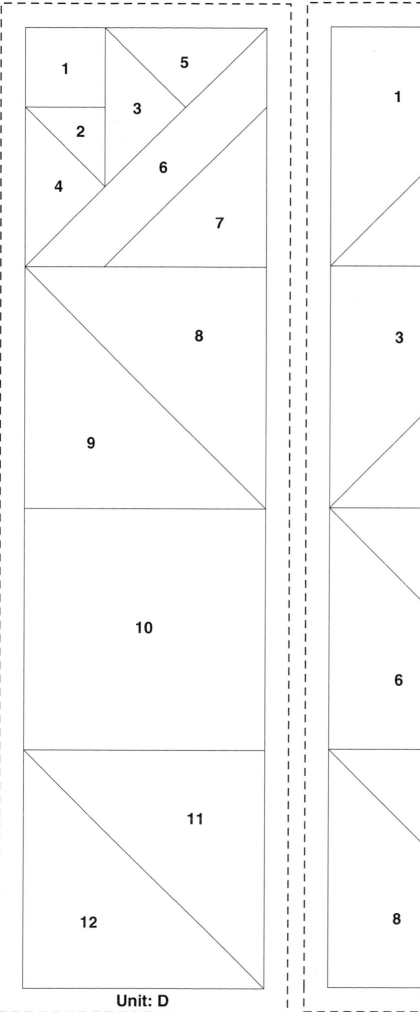

Unit: D

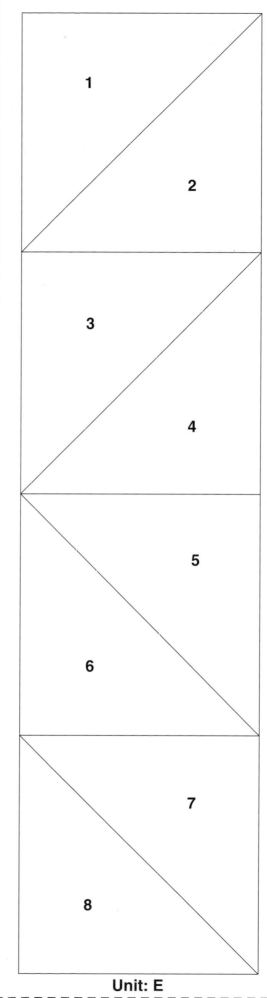

Unit: E

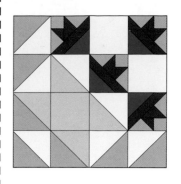

Basket of Lilies 117.

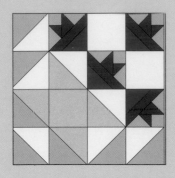

Basket of Lilies
April 1931
The Kansas City Star

When putting the units together, refer to the instructions for the 4" block.

Position Chart — 10" Block

Fabric	Position #	Size	
Unit A – Make 1			
Green Solid	1	1 3/4" x 1 3/4"	
Rose Solid	2,3	2 1/2" x 2 1/2"	◨
Green Solid	4,5	2 1/2" x 2 1/2"	◨
Rose	6	1 1/4" x 4 1/2"	
Green Vine	7	3 1/4" x 3 1/4"	◨
Unit B – Make 1			
Green Solid	1	1 3/4" x 1 3/4"	
Rose Solid	2,3	2 1/2" x 2 1/2"	◨
Green Solid	4,5	2 1/2" x 2 1/2"	◨
Rose	6	1 1/4" x 4 1/2"	
Green Vine	7	3 1/4" x 3 1/4"	◨
Background	8	3 1/4" x 3 1/4"	
Background	9	4" x 4"	◨
Green Solid	10	4" x 4"	◨
Unit C – Make 1			
Green Solid	1	1 3/4" x 1 3/4"	
Rose Solid	2,3	2 1/2" x 2 1/2"	◨
Green Solid	4,5	2 1/2" x 2 1/2"	◨
Rose	6	1 1/4" x 4 1/2"	
Green Vine	7	3 1/4" x 3 1/4"	◨
Background	8	3 1/4" x 3 1/4"	
Background	9,11	4" x 4"	◨
Floral	10	4" x 4"	◨
Green Solid	12	4" x 4"	◨
Unit D - Make 1			
Green Solid	1	1 3/4" x 1 3/4"	
Rose Solid	2,3	2 1/2" x 2 1/2"	◨
Green Solid	4,5	2 1/2" x 2 1/2"	◨
Rose	6	1 1/4" x 4 1/2"	
Green Vine	7	3 1/4" x 3 1/4"	◨
Background	8	4" x 4"	◨
Floral	9,11	4" x 4"	◨
Floral	10	3 1/4" x 3 1/4"	
Green Solid	12	4" x 4"	◨
Unit E - Make 1			
Green Solid	1,3,6,8	4" x 4"	◨
Background	2,4,7	4" x 4"	◨
Floral	5	4" x 4"	◨

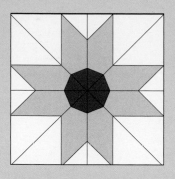

Missouri Daisy
March 1935
The Kansas City Star

Cutting Directions — Missouri Daisy 4" Block

From the light fabric, cut:

■ One 2" x 8" strip. Subcut the strip into four 2" squares. Cut the squares into half-square triangles.

■ One 3" x 12" strip. Subcut the strip into four 3" squares. Cut the squares into half-square triangles.

From the floral fabric, cut:

■ One 1 1/2" x 20" strip. Subcut the strip into eight 1 1/2" x 2 1/2" rectangles.

From the dark fabric, cut:

■ One 1 1/4" x 10" strip. Subcut the strip into eight 1 1/4" squares.

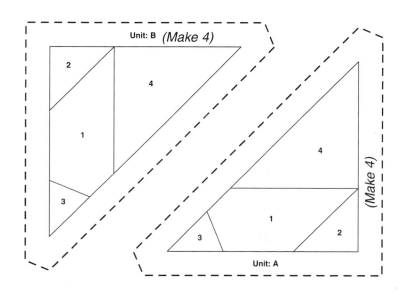

Unit: B *(Make 4)*

2

4

1

3

4

1

3 2

(Make 4)

Unit: A

Missouri Daisy 119.

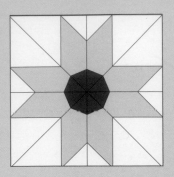

*M*issouri *D*aisy
March 1935
The Kansas City Star

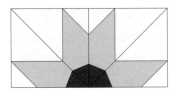

Position Chart

Fabric	Position #	Size	
Unit A – Make 4			
Floral	1	1 1/2" x 2 1/2"	
Light	2	2" x 2"	◧
Dark	3	1 1/4" x 1 1/4"	
Light	4	3" x 3"	◧
Unit B – Make 4			
Floral	1	1 1/2" x 2 1/2"	
Light	2	2" x 2"	◧
Dark	3	1 1/4" x 1 1/4"	
Light	4	3" x 3"	◧

4" Block

ASSEMBLING THE BLOCK:

Sew each Unit A to a Unit B as shown.

Sew the units together as shown to complete the block.

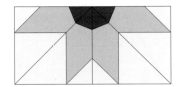
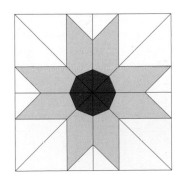

Cutting Directions — Missouri Daisy 10" Block

From the background fabric, cut:

■ One 3 1/4" x 13" strip. Subcut the strip into four 3 1/4" squares. Cut the squares into half-square triangles.

■ One 5" x 20" strip. Subcut the strip into four 5" squares. Cut the squares into half-square triangles.

From the rose fabric, cut:

■ One 2 1/2" x 40" strip. Subcut the strip into eight 2 1/2" x 5" rectangles.

From the yellow fabric, cut:

■ One 2 1/4" x 18" strip. Subcut the strip into eight 2 1/4" squares.

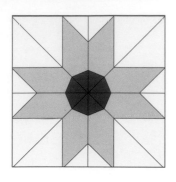

Missouri **D**aisy
March 1935
The Kansas City Star

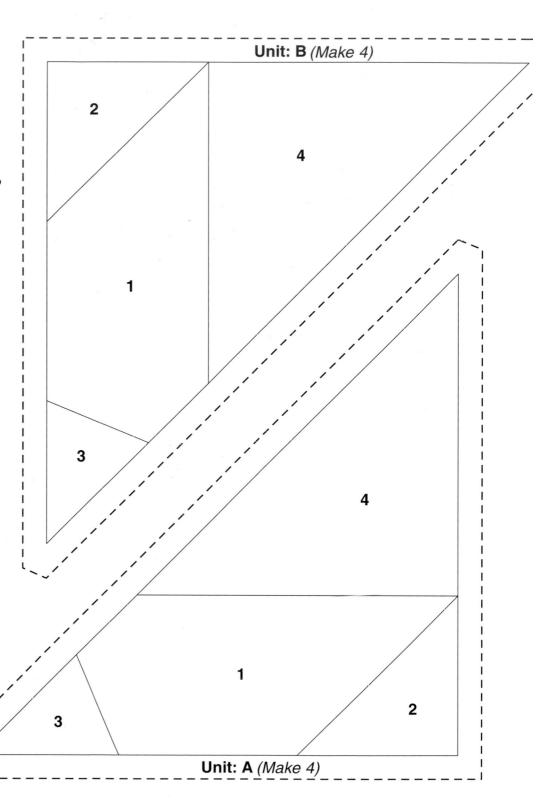

Unit: B *(Make 4)*

2

4

1

3

4

1

3

2

Unit: A *(Make 4)*

Missouri Daisy Garden Apron

Make a gardener's apron... see the instructions for how to make this great garden apron following the instructions on pages 142-143.

10" Block

Fabric	Position #	Size	
Unit A – Make 4			
Rose	1	2 1/2" x 5"	
Background	2	3 1/4" x 3 1/4"	◣
Yellow	3	2 1/4" x 2 1/4"	
Background	4	5" x 5"	◥
Unit B – Make 4			
Rose	1	2 1/2" x 5"	
Background	2	3 1/4" x 3 1/4"	◥
Yellow	3	2 1/4" x 2 1/4"	
Background	4	5" x 5"	◣

When you are ready to sew the units together, follow the instructions given for the 4" block.

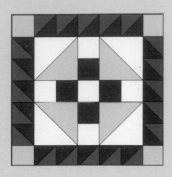

Prickly Pear
October 1931
The Kansas City Star

Cutting Directions — Prickly Pear 4" Block

From the light fabric, cut:

■ One 1 1/2" x 7 1/2" strip. Subcut the strip into five 1 1/2" squares.

■ One 2 1/2" x 5" strip. Subcut the strip into two 2 1/2" squares. Cut the squares into half-square triangles.

From the floral fabric, cut:

■ One 1 1/2" x 6" strip. Subcut the strip into four 1 1/2" squares.

■ One 2 1/2" x 5" strip. Subcut the strip into two 2 1/2" squares. Cut the two squares into half-square triangles.

From the dark rose fabric, cut:

■ One 1 3/4" x 17 1/2" strip. Subcut the strip into ten 1 3/4" squares. Cut the squares into half-square triangles.

From the dark green fabric, cut:

■ One 1 3/4" x 17 1/2" strip. Subcut the strip into ten 1 3/4" squares. Cut the squares into half-square triangles.

■ One 1 1/2" x 6" strip. Subcut the strip into four 1 1/2" squares.

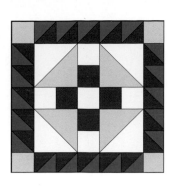

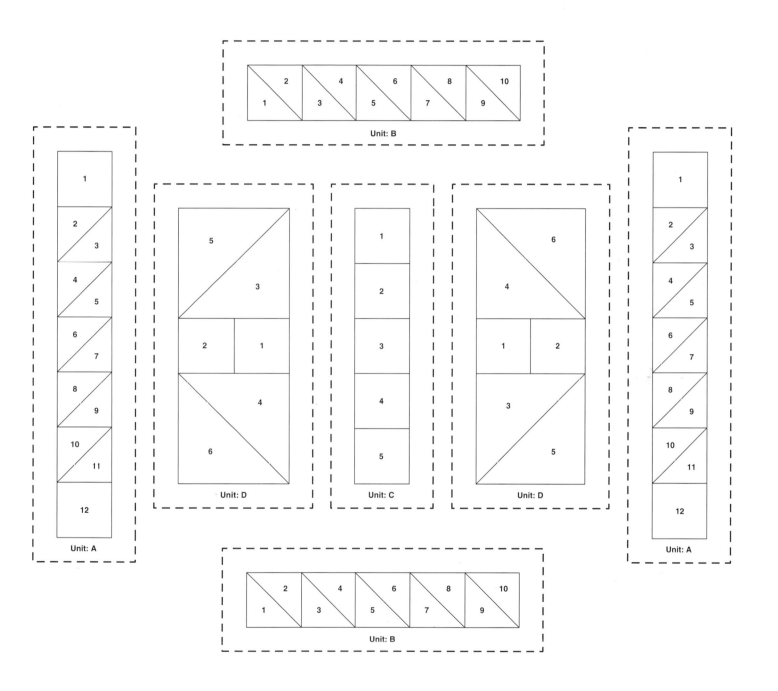

Unit: B

Unit: A

Unit: D

Unit: C

Unit: D

Unit: A

Unit: B

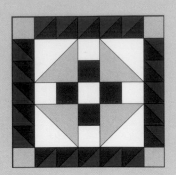

Prickly Pear
October 1931
The Kansas City Star

	Fabric	Position #	Size
			4" Block
Unit A – Make 2			
	Floral	1,12	1 1/2" x 1 1/2"
	Dark Rose	2,4,6,8,10	1 3/4" x 1 3/4"
	Green	3,5,7,9,11	1 3/4" x 1 3/4"
Unit B – Make 2			
	Green	1,3,5,7,9	1 3/4" x 1 3/4"
	Dark Rose	2,4,6,8,10	1 3/4" x 1 3/4"
Unit C – Make 1			
	Light	1,3,5	1 1/2" x 1 1/2"
	Green	2,4	1 1/2" x 1 1/2"
Unit D – Make 2			
	Green	1	1 1/2" x 1 1/2"
	Light	2	1 1/2" x 1 1/2"
	Floral	3,4	2 1/2" x 2 1/2"
	Light	5,6	2 1/2" x 2 1/2"

ASSEMBLING THE BLOCK:

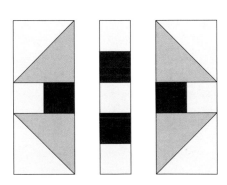

Sew a Unit D to either side of a Unit C as shown.

Sew the Unit Bs to the top and bottom of the block.

To complete the block sew a Unit A to either side as shown.

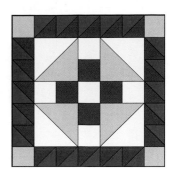

Cutting Directions — Prickly Pear 10" Block

From the background fabric, cut:

■ One 2 1/4" x 11 1/4" strip. Subcut the strip into five 2 1/4" squares.

■ One 4 1/4" x 8 1/2" strip. Subcut the strip into two 4 1/4" squares. Cut the squares into half-square triangles.

From the floral fabric, cut:

■ One 2 1/4" x 9" strip. Subcut the strip into four 2 1/4" squares.

■ One 4 1/4" x 8 1/2" strip. Subcut the strip into two 4 1/4" squares. Cut the squares into half-square triangles.

From the rose fabric, cut:

■ One 2 3/4" x 27 1/2" strip. Subcut the strip into ten 2 3/4" squares. Cut the squares into half-square triangles.

From the green fabric, cut:

■ One 2 3/4" x 27 1/2" strip. Subcut the strip into ten 2 3/4" squares. Cut the squares into half-square triangles.

■ One 2 1/4" x 9" strip. Subcut the strip into four 2 1/4" squares.

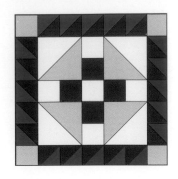

Prickly **P**ear
October 1931
The Kansas City
Star

(Make 2)

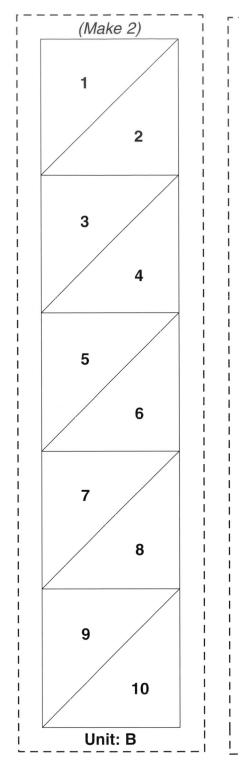

1

2

3

4

5

6

7

8

9

10

Unit: B

(Make 2)

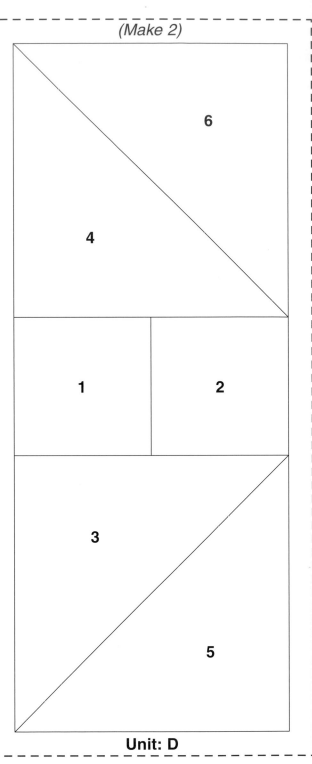

6

4

1

2

3

5

Unit: D

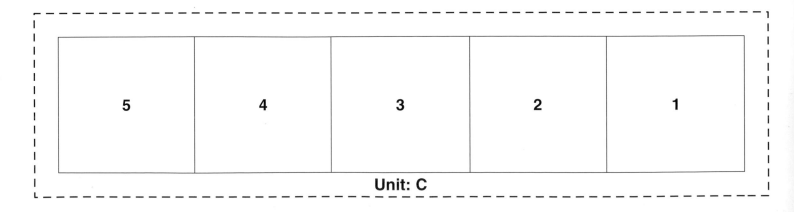

5 | 4 | 3 | 2 | 1

Unit: C

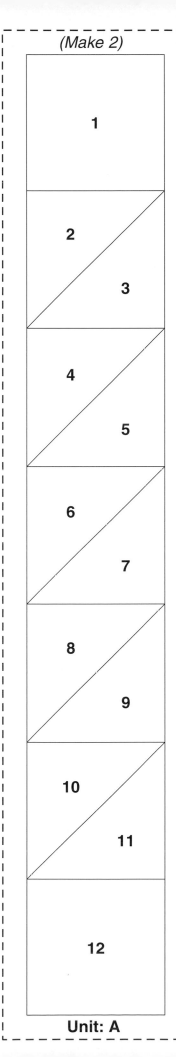

(Make 2)

1
2 / 3
4 / 5
6 / 7
8 / 9
10 / 11
12

Unit: A

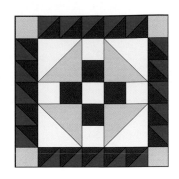

Position Chart — 10" Block

Fabric	Position #	Size	
Unit A – Make 2			
Floral	1,12	2 1/4" x 2 1/4"	
Rose Solid	2,4,6,8,10	2 3/4" x 2 3/4"	◣
Green Vine	3,5,7,9,11	2 3/4" x 2 3/4"	◣
Unit B – Make 2			
Green Vine	1,3,5,7,9	2 3/4" x 2 3/4"	◣
Rose Solid	2,4,6,8,10	2 3/4" x 2 3/4"	�
Unit C – Make 1			
Background	1,3,5	2 1/4" x 2 1/4"	
Green Vine	2,4	2 1/4" x 2 1/4"	
Unit D – Make 2			
Green Vine	1	2 1/4" x 2 1/4"	
Background	2	2 1/4" x 2 1/4"	
Floral	3,4	4 1/4" x 4 1/4"	◣
Background	5,6	4 1/4" x 4 1/4"	◣

When you are ready to sew the units together, refer to the directions for the 4" block.

*P*oinsettia
December 1931
The Kansas City Star

Cutting Directions — Poinsettia 4" Block:

From the light fabric, cut:

■ One 1 1/2" x 24" strip. Subcut the strip into sixteen 1 1/2" squares. Cut twelve of the squares into half-square triangles. You should have 24 triangles and four 1 1/2" squares.

■ One 3/4" x 10" strip. Subcut the strip into eight 3/4" x 1 1/4" rectangles.

■ One 1 1/4" x 18" strip. Subcut the strip into four 1 1/4" x 2 rectangles and eight 1 1/4" squares.

■ One 3" x 6" strip. Subcut the strip into two 3" squares. Cut the squares into half-square triangles.

From the dark rose fabric, cut:

■ One 1 1/2" x 6" strip. Subcut the strip into four 1 1/2" squares. Cut the squares into half-square triangles.

■ Cut one 1" x 10" strip. Subcut the strip into four 1" x 2 1/2" rectangles.

From the dark green fabric, cut:

■ One 1 1/2" x 2 1/2" strip. Subcut the strip into two 1 1/2" squares. Cut the squares into half-square triangles.

■ One 1" x 18" strip. Subcut the strip into eight 1" x 1 3/4" rectangles and four 1" squares.

■ One 1 1/4" x 2 1/2" strip. Subcut the strip into two 1 1/4" squares.

■ One 1" x 2" strip.

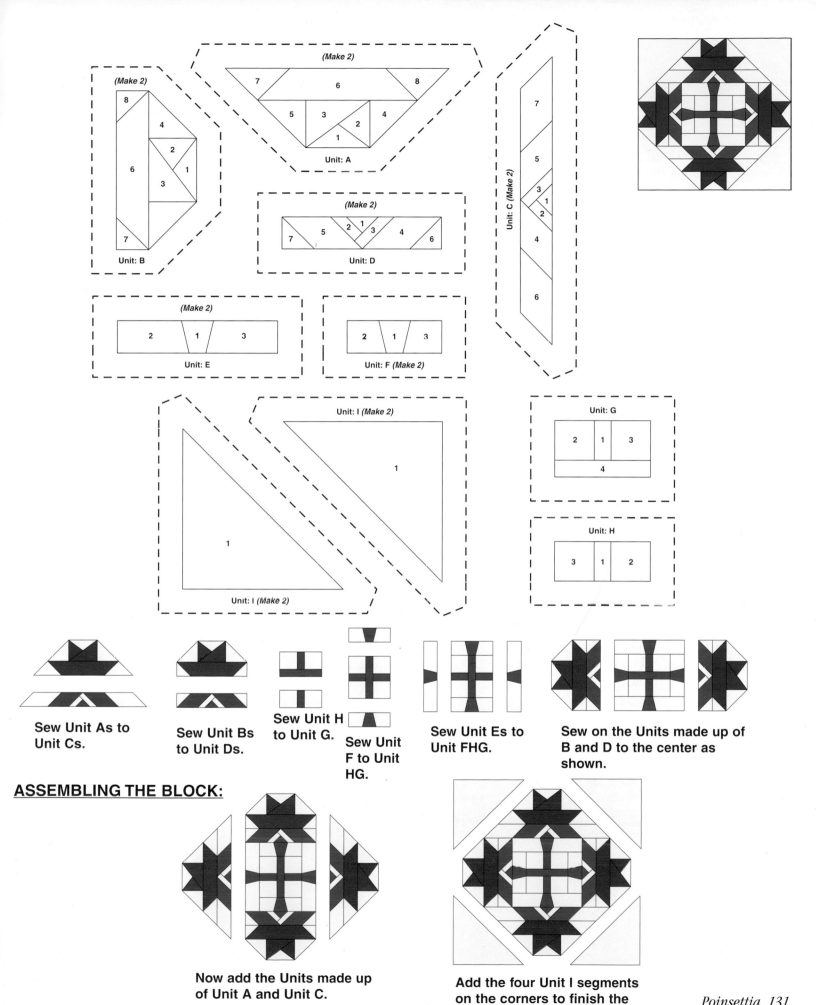

(Make 2)

Unit: A

(Make 2)

Unit: B

(Make 2)

Unit: C *(Make 2)*

(Make 2)

Unit: D

(Make 2)

Unit: E

Unit: F *(Make 2)*

Unit: I *(Make 2)*

Unit: I *(Make 2)*

Unit: G

Unit: H

Sew Unit As to Unit Cs.

Sew Unit Bs to Unit Ds.

Sew Unit H to Unit G.

Sew Unit F to Unit HG.

Sew Unit Es to Unit FHG.

Sew on the Units made up of B and D to the center as shown.

ASSEMBLING THE BLOCK:

Now add the Units made up of Unit A and Unit C.

Add the four Unit I segments on the corners to finish the block.

Poinsettia 131.

*P*oinsettia

December 1931

The Kansas City Star

Position Chart

	Fabric	Position #	Size	4" Block
Unit A – Make 2				
	Light	1,4,5,7,8	1 1/2" x 1 1/2"	◣
	Dark Rose	2,3	1 1/2" x 1 1/2"	◣
	Dark Rose	6	1" x 2 1/2"	
Unit B – Make 2				
	Light	1,4,5,7,8	1 1/2" x 1 1/2"	◣
	Dark Rose	2,3	1 1/2" x 1 1/2"	◣
	Dark Rose	6	1" x 2 1/2"	
Unit C – Make 2				
	Dark Green	1	1 1/2" x 1 1/2"	◣
	Light	2,3	3/4" x 1 1/4"	
	Dark Green	4,5	1" x 1 3/4"	
	Light	6,7	2" x 1 1/4"	
Unit D – Make 2				
	Dark Green	1	1 1/2" x 1 1/2"	◣
	Light	2,3	3/4" x 1 1/4"	
	Dark Green	4,5	1" x 1 3/4"	
	Light	6,7	1 1/2" x 1 1/2"	◣
Unit E – Make 2				
	Dark Green	1	1" x 1"	
	Light	2,3	1 1/2" x 1 1/2"	
Unit F – Make 2				
	Dark Green	1	1" x 1"	
	Light	2,3	1 1/4" x 1 1/4"	
Unit G - Make 1				
	Dark Green	1	1 1/4" x 1 1/4"	
	Light	2,3	1 1/4" x 1 1/4"	
	Dark Green	4	1" x 2"	
Unit H - Make 1				
	Dark Green	1	1 1/4" x 1 1/4"	
	Light	2,3	1 1/4" x 1 1/4"	
Unit I - Make 4				
	Light	1	3" x 3"	◣

Cutting Directions — Poinsettia 10" Block

From the background fabric, cut:

■ One 2 3/4" x 33" strip. Subcut the strip into twelve 2 3/4" squares. Cut the squares into half-square triangles.

■ One 1" x 18" strip. Subcut the strip into eight 1" x 2 1/4" rectangles.

■ One 2" x 14" strip. Subcut the strip into four 2" x 3 1/2" rectangles.

■ One 1 3/4" x 16" strip. Subcut the strip into four 1 3/4" squares and four 1 3/4" x 2 1/4" rectangles.

■ One 2 1/2" x 12" strip. Subcut the strip into four 2 1/2" x 3" rectangles.

■ One 6" x 12" strip. Subcut the strip into two 6" squares. Cut the squares into half-square triangles.

From the rose fabric, cut:

■ One 2 3/4" x 11" strip. Subcut the strip into four 2 3/4" squares. Cut the squares into half-square triangles.

■ One 1 1/2" x 23" strip. Subcut the strip into four 1 1/2" x 5 3/4" rectangles.

From the green fabric, cut:

■ One 2 1/4" x 4 1/2" strip. Subcut the strip into two 2 1/4" squares. Cut the squares into half-square triangles.

■ One 1 3/4" x 33" strip. Subcut the strip into eight 1 3/4" x 3 1/4" rectangles and four 1 3/4" squares.

■ One 1 1/4" x 6 3/4" strip. Subcut the strip into one 1 1/4" x 3 1/4" rectangle and two 1 1/4" x 1 3/4" rectangles.

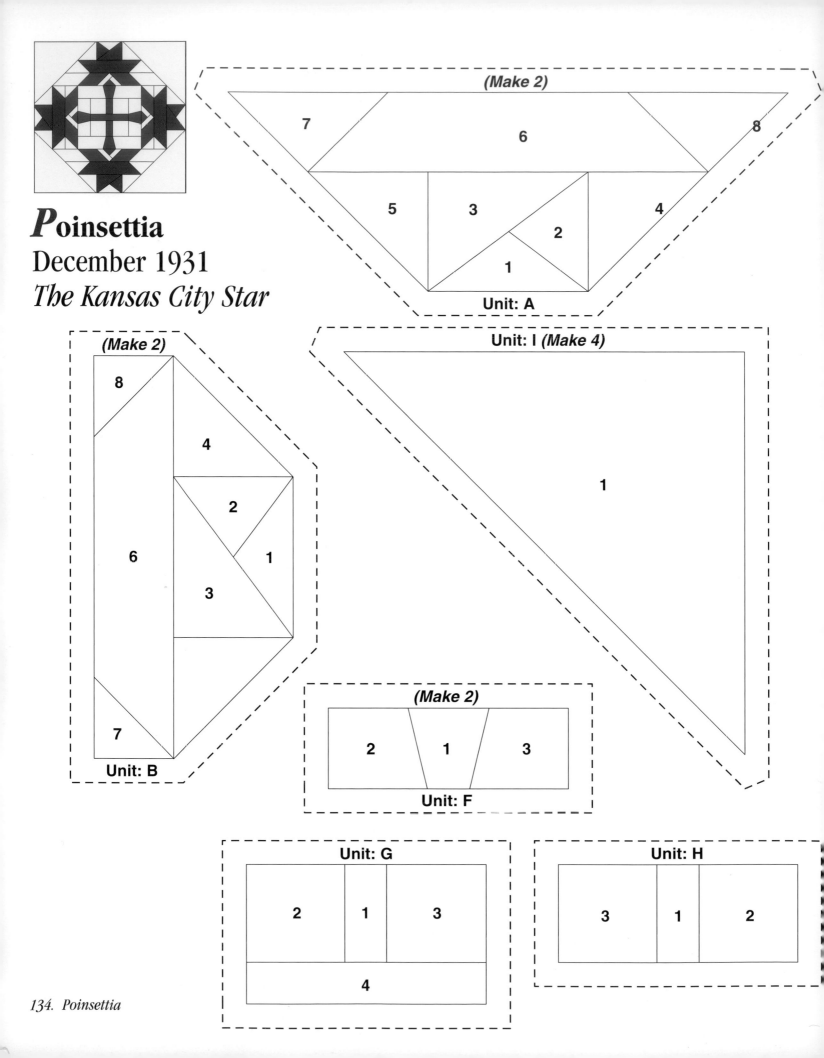

*P*oinsettia

December 1931
The Kansas City Star

(Make 2)

7   6   8
5   3   4
2
1

Unit: A

Unit: I (Make 4)

1

(Make 2)

8
4
2
6   1
3
7

Unit: B

(Make 2)

2   1   3

Unit: F

Unit: G

2   1   3
4

Unit: H

3   1   2

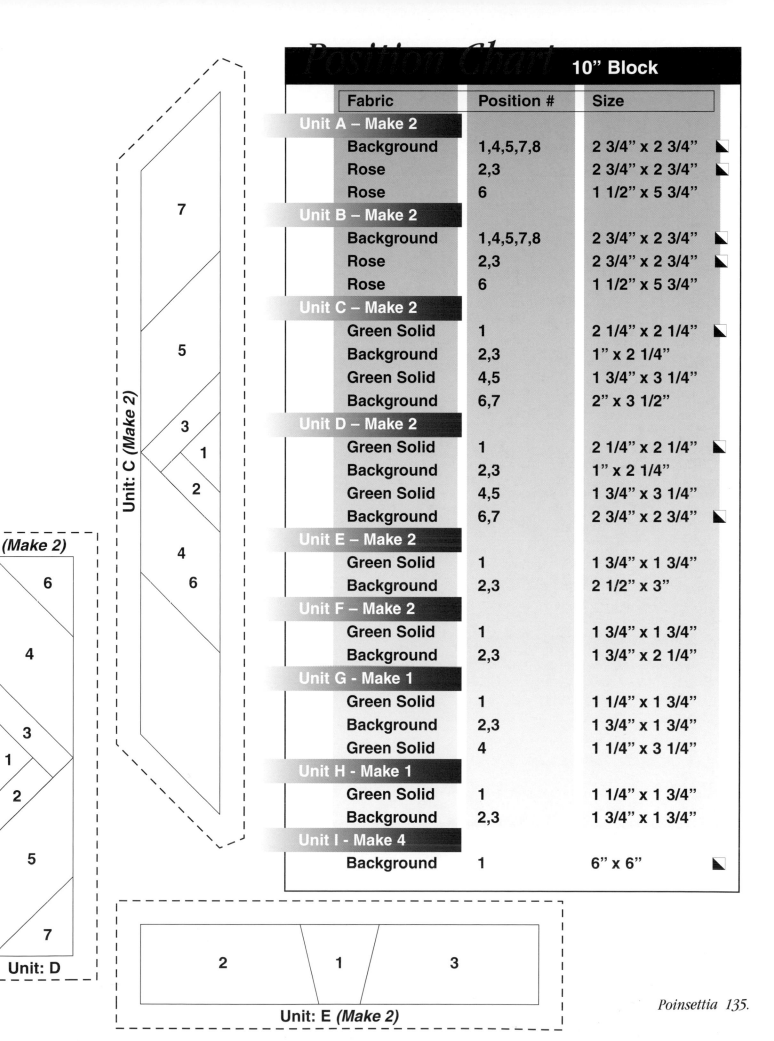

Position Chart — 10" Block

Fabric	Position #	Size
Unit A – Make 2		
Background	1,4,5,7,8	2 3/4" x 2 3/4"
Rose	2,3	2 3/4" x 2 3/4"
Rose	6	1 1/2" x 5 3/4"
Unit B – Make 2		
Background	1,4,5,7,8	2 3/4" x 2 3/4"
Rose	2,3	2 3/4" x 2 3/4"
Rose	6	1 1/2" x 5 3/4"
Unit C – Make 2		
Green Solid	1	2 1/4" x 2 1/4"
Background	2,3	1" x 2 1/4"
Green Solid	4,5	1 3/4" x 3 1/4"
Background	6,7	2" x 3 1/2"
Unit D – Make 2		
Green Solid	1	2 1/4" x 2 1/4"
Background	2,3	1" x 2 1/4"
Green Solid	4,5	1 3/4" x 3 1/4"
Background	6,7	2 3/4" x 2 3/4"
Unit E – Make 2		
Green Solid	1	1 3/4" x 1 3/4"
Background	2,3	2 1/2" x 3"
Unit F – Make 2		
Green Solid	1	1 3/4" x 1 3/4"
Background	2,3	1 3/4" x 2 1/4"
Unit G - Make 1		
Green Solid	1	1 1/4" x 1 3/4"
Background	2,3	1 3/4" x 1 3/4"
Green Solid	4	1 1/4" x 3 1/4"
Unit H - Make 1		
Green Solid	1	1 1/4" x 1 3/4"
Background	2,3	1 3/4" x 1 3/4"
Unit I - Make 4		
Background	1	6" x 6"

Unit: C *(Make 2)*

7
5
3
1
2
4
6

(Make 2)

6
4
3
1
2
5
7

Unit: D

2 1 3

Unit: E *(Make 2)*

Poinsettia 135.

Carolyn's Paper-Pieced Garden was pieced by Carolyn Cullinan McCormick. Tracy Peterson Yadon, Lady Quilter of Manhattan, Montana, did the quilting.

Putting it all Together

Carolyn's Paper-Pieced Garden

Fabric Requirements:

■ **Blocks:**

Floral	1 yard
Rose Solid	2 yards
Rose Leaves	2 yards
Green Twig	2 yards
Green Solid	2 yards
Background	3 yards
Green Leaves	1/4 yard
Yellow	1/4 yard
Brown	1/8 yard

■ **Background** — 2 1/2 yards

■ **1st Border:**
   Green Solid — 1/2 yard

■ **2nd Border:**
   Floral — 1 1/4 yard

■ **Binding:**
   Green Solid — 3/4 yard

■ **Backing:** — 5 yards

■ **Batting (90" wide):** 2 1/2 yards

The fabric requirements are generous. You may wish to use different fabrics for each block.

To Make the Quilt:

From the background fabric cut the following pieces:

■ **Solid Blocks:**
Cut four 10 1/2" strips the width of the fabric. Subcut the strips cut into 10 1/2" squares. You will need 12 squares.

■ **Setting Triangles:**
Cut four 15 3/8" squares. Cut on the diagonal from corner to corner twice, each square will give you 4 quarter-square triangles. You will need 14 setting triangles.

■ **Setting Corner Triangles:**
Cut two 8" squares. Cut the squares on the diagonal from corner to corner. Each square will give you 2 triangles.

You will need 4 of these triangles.

Sew the quilt blocks together using the solid blocks, setting triangles and setting corner triangles.

■ For the first border, cut seven 2" strips the width of the fabric.

■ For the second border, cut eight 5" strips the width of the fabric.

Sew the borders on the top, bottom and sides of the quilt.

Carolyn's Paper-Pieced Garden in Miniature

Pictured: This quilt, using the 4" blocks, was pieced and quilted by Carolyn Cullinan McCormick.

Fabric Requirements:

Blocks:

Floral	1/2 yard
Dark Burgundy	3/8 yard
Medium rose	3/8 yard
Dark Green	1/2 yard
Background	1 yard

Solid Blocks:

Background	5/8 yards

Border:

Background	3/8 yard

Binding:

Green	1/4 yard
Backing:	1 yard
Batting:	1 yard

(The fabric requirements are estimated, you may wish to use different fabric for each block.)

To Make the Quilt:

From the background fabric cut the following pieces.

Solid Blocks:
Cut two 4 1/2" strips the width of the fabric. Subcut the strips into 4 1/2" squares. You will need 12 squares.

Setting Triangles:
Cut one 6 7/8" strip the width of the fabric. From the strip cut four 6 7/8" squares. Cut on the diagonal from corner to corner twice. Each square will give you 4 pieces. You will need 14 setting triangles.

Setting Corner Triangles:
Cut two 3 3/4" squares. Cut the squares on the diagonal from corner to corner. Each square will give you 2 triangles. You will need 4 triangles.

Sew the quilt blocks together using the solid blocks, setting triangles, and setting corner triangles.

For the border, cut four 2" strips the width of the fabric and sew them on to the sides and top and bottom of the quilt.

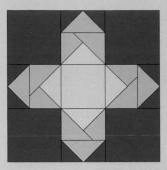

Leaves and Flowers
August 1935
The Kansas City Star

Carolyn Cullinan McCormick made this table runner using the Leaves and Flower pattern.

Leaves and Flowers Table Runner

Supplies –

- 3- 10" blocks of your choice
- Sashing fabric - 3/8 yard
- Setting Triangles - 1 yard
- Binding - 3/8 yard
- Backing - 1 1/4 yard
- Batting - 21" x 56"
- Thread

Leaves and Flowers Table Runner

Cutting Directions:

From the sashing fabric:

■ Cut six 2" x 10 1/2" rectangles.
■ Cut six 2" x 13 1/2" rectangles

For the setting triangles:

■ Cut one 19 5/8" square.
■ Subcut the square into quarter-square triangles as shown.

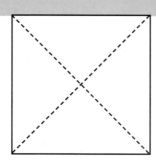

■ Cut two 10 1/8" squares. Subcut the squares into half-square triangles as shown.

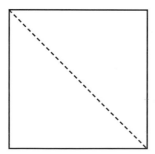

For the binding:

■ Cut four 2 1/2" x 45" strips.

Sewing Directions:

1. Sew the sashing onto all sides of the blocks, pressing as you go.

2. Remove the paper from the blocks.

3. Sew the blocks and the setting triangles together.

4. Sew on the corner triangles.

5. Pin or baste the backing, batting and top together.

6. Quilt as desired and sew on the binding to complete the runner.

May Basket in Floral Tones

September 1947
The Kansas City Star

May Basket in Floral Tones Tote Bag

Supplies –

- 1 yard denim or canvas
- 1- 10" block
- 1/2 yard of complimentary fabric
- 1 yard belt webbing
- Thread

The May Basket in Floral Tones Tote bag, pictured, was made by Carolyn Cullinan McCormick.

May Basket Tote Bag

Cutting Directions:

From the denim:

■ Cut one 16" x 34" rectangle.

From the complimentary fabric:

■ Cut one 10 1/2" x 10 1/2" square of backing fabric for the block.

■ Cut two 2" x 16" rectangles for the top border.

■ Cut two 2" x 18" rectangles for handles.

Belt webbing: 2- 18" long

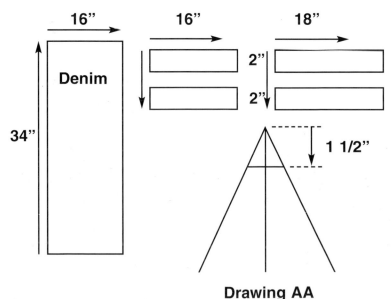

Drawing AA

1. To make the handles, fold the complimentary fabric in half, right sides together, stitch using a 1/4" seam allowance. Trim to 1/8". Turn right side out using a bodkin and straw. Press, leaving the seam down the center. Place the fabric down the center of the belt webbing and stitch on both sides.

2. Along the top edge of the tote bag, on the front, measure down 1 1/4" and mark lightly with a pencil. Place the raw edge of the complimentary fabric (right side down) on the pencil line. Sew using 1/4" seam allowance. Press to the top of the bag. Turn the raw edge of the complimentary fabric and denim over 3/8" and press. Fold over 5/8"and press. Do not sew yet.

3. Place the backing fabric (right sides together) on the 10" block. Stitch, leaving an opening to turn right side out. Remove the paper from the back of the block, trim the corners, turn right side out, and press. Hand stitch the opening. Center the block at the top of the front directly below the trim of the complimentary fabric. Stitch into place.

4. Place the handles 3 1/2" from each edge under the 5/8" seam allowance. Stitch around the top sewing in the handles. Pull the handles to the top and double stitch.

5. Fold the bag right sides together, matching the top. Pin in place. Stitch both sides using 1/4" seam allowance. Zigzag or serge the raw edge.

6. Match the center bottom and one side seam, making sure the fabric is flat. Pin in place. From the point measure down 1 1/2". Mark lightly with a pencil. Stitch on the line. Trim seam allowance down to 1/4". Zigzag or serge the raw edge. Follow the same procedure for the other side. (See the drawing to the left marked AA).

7. Turn bag right side out. Eureka! You have a quilting bag.